The Struggle for Federal Aid
First Phase

A HISTORY OF THE ATTEMPTS TO OBTAIN
FEDERAL AID FOR THE COMMON SCHOOLS
1870-1890

By GORDON CANFIELD LEE, Ph.D.

ASSISTANT PROFESSOR OF EDUCATION AND HEAD OF
THE DEPARTMENT, POMONA COLLEGE
CLAREMONT, CALIFORNIA

Teachers College, Columbia University
Contributions to Education, No. 957

BUREAU OF PUBLICATIONS
TEACHERS COLLEGE, COLUMBIA UNIVERSITY
NEW YORK, 1949

Library of Congress Cataloging in Publication Data

Lee, Gordon Canfield, 1916-
  The struggle for Federal aid, first phase.

  Reprint of the 1949 ed., issued in series: Teachers
College, Columbia University. Contributions to education, no. 957.
  Originally presented as the author's thesis, Columbia.
  Bibliography: p.
  1. Federal aid to education--History. 2. Education
and state--United States. 3. Educational law and le-
gislation--United States. I. Title. II. Series: Columbia University, Teachers College. Contributions to
education, no. 957.
LB2825.L38 1972   379'.12'0973   79-176979

ISBN 0-404-55957-3

From the edition of 1949, New York
First AMS edition published in 1972
Manufactured in the United States

AMS PRESS, INC.
NEW YORK, N. Y.   10003

TO
GRACE
and
EDNA and ED

ACKNOWLEDGMENTS

IT IS IMPOSSIBLE to indicate adequately the extent of my indebtedness to those who have assisted in bringing this work to completion: to Dr. George S. Counts, sponsor of the study, and to Dr. R. Freeman Butts, both of Teachers College, Columbia University, for continuous guidance, generous criticism and encouragement, and a personal relationship of warmth and kindliness; to Drs. Edmund deS. Brunner, Edward H. Reisner, and Ryland W. Crary, Teachers College, Columbia University, all of whom have given freely of their time and counsel; to Dean Harry J. Carman of Columbia College and to Dr. John A. Krout of Columbia University for valuable criticism and suggestions; to Dr. Erling Hunt, also of Teachers College, whose excellent and exciting instruction in historiography and research techniques has for a decade proved of great value to me; to a fellow student, Lawrence A. Cremin, for his constant interest and support. Finally, no words can convey the extent to which this study is the product of my wife's patience, insight, and unfailing confidence.

GORDON CANFIELD LEE

Teachers College
Columbia University
May, 1948

CONTENTS

ix

The Struggle for Federal Aid
First Phase

· I ·

INTRODUCTION

THIS study developed out of a deep interest in the problem of federal aid to education and the allied question of the interrelationship of education and politics. With the repeated contemporary attempts to enact legislation granting federal aid to general public education, the questions arose: What, in the legislative history of the United States, is of significance in revealing the character of earlier attempts to obtain such aid? Has federal participation in education of the nature now being proposed been considered before, and if so, what were the details of those proposals and how were they dealt with? What forces promoted and what interests blocked the enactment of such legislation? And finally, do these earlier experiences have any meanings for the efforts now (1948) being made in this area?

This interrogation inevitably led to the discovery that the twenty years immediately following the Civil War stands as the period of most extensive demand for and intensive consideration of the provision of federal aid for the common schools prior to the 1920's. In some respects, the years 1870 to 1890, with which this investigation is concerned, represent the peak of legislative and public activity with regard to this question.

The development of federal aid to education in the United States has not yet been presented in a unified, integrated historical analysis. The most notable work that has been done so far is contained in such studies as those of Blackmar and Kandel, and certain of the publications of the United States Office of Education. Blackmar's *The History of Federal and State Aid to Higher Education*, though published in 1894, still stands as an able and complete summary of the development of aid to higher education up to that time, but it contains only slight references to the question of aid to the common schools. Professor Kandel's excellent and fascinating study of *Federal Aid for Vocational Education* is an extremely valuable reference for anyone concerned with the history of any aspect of federal aid legislation, but here the emphasis is on aid to a particular segment of public education and only incidental attention is paid to the problem of general aid to the public schools. Numerous bulletins and circulars of the Office of Education outline the history of federal aid to education in terms of the specifics of legislation that has been enacted (i.e. Keesecker's *Digest of Legislation Providing Federal Subsidies for Education*, U. S. Office of Education Bulletin No. 8, 1930), but these are in no sense analytical studies. Thus, the conclusion is inescapable that the history of attempts to obtain federal aid for general public education has received very scant attention.

This investigation is concerned with the attempts to enact such legislation between 1870 and 1890. It seems clear that at no time in the nation's history before the 1930's has the need for federal support of education been as acute, as widespread, and as widely recognized as in the years immediately following the Civil War. Thus, it is not surprising to find the first serious Congressional consideration of a proposal of federal participation in common school education occurring in 1870-1871. From then until 1890, the question was, to varying degrees of intensity, constantly before the national legislature and the public, and, with the introduction of the Blair bill in 1884, its consideration in Congress reached as yet unequaled proportions. But, with the final appearance of the Blair bill in 1890, this first chapter in the development of federal aid to common school education was closed, for not until 1919 did a bill with a similar purpose reach the floor of either house of Congress.

This study has proceeded with the following six guiding purposes in view:

1. To analyze the various proposals for federal aid to the common schools which received legislative consideration during the period 1870 to 1890.

2. To describe the Congressional and political party activity with regard to these proposals.

3. To describe the public pressures and interests which favored or opposed such legislation.

4. To discover the arguments presented as bases for approval or opposition.

5. To offer some explanation for the prevalence of such attitudes.

6. To draw implications which might be valid for the contemporary national educational situation.

There remains to be considered a question of definition: What was meant by the term "common schools" as used during this period? The proposed legislation, the debates which such proposals engendered, and the literature of the time, both professional and non-professional, used the expression in a way that seemed to assume general agreement as to its meaning; but nowhere in legislative activity or in the literature was that meaning made explicit. It became evident, as Congressional debate proceeded, that the legal determination of the extent of the "common school" as an institution was to be left to the several states. Nevertheless, some general understanding of the signification of the term was present and seems to have been largely assumed as universal.

Definitions of the term "common school" seem to have been prevalent on three levels. In the first place, the "common school" was described in terms of the extent to which it served the youth of the country, the number of years or grades of school provided. While some disagreement existed here as to the upper limits of the "common" school, the 1870's and 1880's were decades which saw a rapid increase in the demand for and the acceptance of the high school as an integral part of the public school system. The celebrated decisions of the courts of Michigan and Illinois, notably the "Kalamazoo case" of 1874, had established the legal status of the high school as an institution rightfully and legitimately supported by public taxation, hence a part of the public, i.e. the "common" school system.

In the second place, and here much more unanimity of opinion was apparent, the "common school" was viewed as the agency which taught the elementary branches of knowledge— for example, reading, spelling, grammar, arithmetic, geography, and United States history, according to the laws of the state of Illinois. But, unquestionably, the sine qua non of the "common school" in the minds of nearly all people was its *public* character: schools were "common" schools because they were open to all and supported by all. Closely related to this last conception, so closely that for many the relationship was inextricable, was the concept of *local* responsibility for the operation of the "common school."

It is probably not an exaggeration to say that, throughout the development of American education and perhaps most prominently during this period, the term "common schools" reflected a spiritual as well as a physical concept. When a man thought of the "common schools," not only did he bring to mind an established number of grades or a progression from rung to rung on a ladder, but also there was evoked an image of what the school could do for his children and indirectly for his country. While the high school had not yet become firmly rooted in all parts of the United States, the entire country had not only accepted but, as nearly unanimously as is possible for a widespread population, had come to revere and hence to demand the public elementary school.

So it must have been with the legislators. Thus, as they considered the question of federal support of the "common schools," it seems safe to conclude that they conceived those schools to be:

1. open to any who cared to attend, without charge;

2. supported through the medium of general public taxation;

3. locally and publicly controlled; and

4. responsible for instruction in the basic branches of knowledge.

An analysis of this twenty-year period in the development of the idea of federal aid to general education is logically divided into three parts. Congress was concerned, essentially, with legislation involving three patterns of federal participation in public education. The first pattern was epitomized by the Hoar bill (1870-1871), which provided for the establishment of a national system of education. Chapter III, after briefly surveying the economic and resultant educational conditions prevailing in the United States and primarily in the South, focuses upon this proposal. The second pattern, to which Chapter IV is devoted, was one of supporting common school education from the proceeds of the sales of public lands. Legislation of this character was under Congressional consideration from 1872 to 1880. The third basic pattern of federal participation in education was that of appropriating money directly from the national treasury in support of common schools. Chapters V and VI deal exclusively, as did the Congress from 1882 to 1890, with the Blair bill, which proposed this method of providing federal aid. Chapter II is an attempt to present the status of public opinion, national educational legislation, and legislative precedent with regard to the question of federal aid as it existed in 1870. For this chapter, no claim to originality is maintained and the reliance upon earlier scholarship is hereby freely and gratefully acknowledged. Finally, Chapter VII presents a summation of the dominant trends, ideas, and forces which were operative in this area throughout the period under investigation and offers certain implications for contemporary considerations of the problem of federal aid to education.

· *II* ·

THE ESTABLISHMENT OF THE PRECEDENTS: A SURVEY OF THE EXTENSION OF FEDERAL AID TO EDUCATION, 1785-1870

THE BEGINNINGS OF PUBLIC CONCERN OVER FEDERAL AID TO EDUCATION

ANY attempt to determine the exact point at which public opinion crystallizes into public action is subject to challenge. It is possible, however, to note the appearance of specific public pressures or demonstrations and to describe the backlog of tradition and policy which was instrumental in producing the overt manifestations. So it is with the history of federal aid to education in America.

Much has been made of the omission of any specific mention of education from the Constitution of the United States. In Congressional debate, historical analysis, and editorial comment, this fact has been used to demonstrate the incompatibility of the principle of federal aid to education with the American political system. But, in recreating the philosophical climate in which all such expressions have been made, it is important to note that not only suggestions for, but enactments of federal aid legislation antedated the Constitution—that, in fact, many of the men who participated in the creation of the Constitution committed themselves quite definitely to this principle. It is the function of this introductory chapter (1) to describe briefly the accumulation of opinion regarding federal aid which was available to the public and its representatives by 1870, (2) to indicate those points at which definite public pressure became active, and (3)

6

to summarize the major federal aid and allied educational legislation by which certain precedents were established and the stage was set for the struggles of 1870 to 1890.

Perhaps the first suggestion that the national government aid education was made by Colonel Timothy Pickering in 1783. This is contained in his proposals for the settlement of the Ohio territory by veterans of the Revolutionary War. Article 7 of these proposals states that "all the surplus lands shall be the common property of the State and be disposed of for the common good; as for laying out roads, creating public buildings, establishing schools and academies. . . ."[1]

There is much in the writings and speeches of George Washington that lends weight to arguments in favor of federal aid. The Farewell Address has often been cited as indicating what should be implied from the Constitution regarding education. There Washington advised: "Promote, then, as an object of primary importance, institutions for the general diffusion of knowledge. In proportion as the structure of the government gives force to public opinion, it is essential that public opinion be enlightened." Blackmar considers that Washington's private correspondence indicates his advocacy of federal participation in education, specifically with regard to the establishment of a national university. This interest, says Blackmar, sprang from three basic concerns. First, Washington wished to encourage a strictly American rather than a European education. Second, he saw in nationally sponsored education a means of eliminating sectional or local prejudices. And third, as indicated in the Farewell Address, Washington considered "the promotion of political intelligence as a national safeguard."[2]

Washington was not alone of early American political leaders to take such a view. Both Jefferson and Madison recommended Constitutional amendments which would grant some control of education to the Federal Government, although it appears that their interest in such federal participation went no further than

[1] Ellwood P. Cubberley, *State School Administration: A Textbook of Principles*, 19.

[2] Frank W. Blackmar, *The History of Federal and State Aid to Higher Education*, 31.

the subsidization of a national institution of higher learning. James Monroe, in his first annual message in 1817, while discussing internal improvements and public lands, recommended an amendment to the Constitution which would allow Congress to participate in the provision of such improvements. These were to include, he noted, "seminaries for the all-important purpose of diffusing knowledge. . . ."[3]

Expressions such as these were not confined to occupants of the Presidential chair. In 1826, the Committee on Public Lands of the House of Representatives issued a favorable report on a resolution requesting land grants for education.[4] And in 1838, William C. Johnson of Maryland called for land grants "to all the States and Territories of the Union for the purpose of free schools, academies, and the promotion and diffusion of education in every part of the United States."[5] A somewhat different approach is typified by the resolution submitted to Congress in 1854 by Representative Wentworth of Illinois, asking the House Committee on Agriculture to investigate the feasibility and desirability of establishing "a national agricultural school" in conjunction with the Smithsonian Institution.[6]

Political philosophers were not silent on the question of the relationship of national governments to the provision of education. There were doubtless many nineteenth century Americans for whom the following statement in John Stuart Mill's *Political Economy* (1848) carried considerable weight. Mill wrote:

Education, therefore, is one of those things, which it is admissible in principle that a government should provide for the people. The case is one to which the reasons of the noninterference principle do not necessarily or universally extend.

With regard to elementary education, the exception to ordinary rules may, I conceive, justifiably be carried still further. There are certain primary elements and means of knowledge, which . . . all human beings . . . should acquire during childhood. . . . It is there-

[3]James D. Richardson, *A Compilation of the Messages and Papers of the Presidents*, 1789-1879, II, 18.
[4]Cubberley, *op. cit.*, 29.
[5]William C. Johnson, *Public Lands for Educational Purposes*, reprint of speech in House of Representatives, 1838.
[6]Frederick B. Mumford, *The Land Grant College Movement*, 18.

fore an allowable exercise of government, to impose on parents the legal obligation of giving elementary instruction to children. This, however, cannot fairly be done, without taking measures to insure that such instruction shall always be accessible to them, either gratuitously or at a trifling expense.[7]

It would be a mistake to conclude that, before 1870, the totality of expression concerning federal aid to education was favorable. While it is probably true that, in the history of the development of public opinion on any issue, the affirmative expressions precede the negative, this period was not without its champions of the opposition. Perhaps the epitome of this attitude is contained in the statement of President Buchanan when, in 1859, he vetoed the first attempt to apply the proceeds of the sales of public lands to the support of colleges of agriculture and mechanic arts. On this occasion he wrote to Congress: "I deem it to be both inexpedient and unconstitutional." His reasons for the veto were as follows:

1. Such gifts of land would so depress the sale price of public lands as to produce a serious loss in government revenue.

2. Operation on this principle would contribute to the deterioration of the relationship between the states and the Federal Government by permitting the states an enlarged dependence upon federal support.

3. Such a procedure would enhance the possibility of large-scale speculation in land.

4. Since, after so donating the public lands, the Federal Government has no authority to enter the states and enforce the proper use of the proceeds, there would be no guarantee that the purposes of the bill would be served.

5. This legislation would be prejudicial to the interests of existing colleges. (Buchanan here suggested a direct grant to these institutions for the endowment of professorships in the desired areas.)

6. "Congress does not possess the power to appropriate money in the treasury, raised by taxes on the people of the United

[7]John Stuart Mill, *Political Economy*, IX, 8, as quoted in *American Journal of Education*, 13 : 720, 1863.

States, for the purpose of educating the people of the respective states."[8]

Many felt, and continued to feel, with Buchanan that this was not an area for federal activity. On July 7, 1866, the Senate Judiciary Committee, to whom (since there was then no committee on education) had been referred petitions requesting legislation for educational assistance, found itself unable to act. Its report to the Senate stated in part that "while the Committee would be very desirous to pass a law that would accomplish that object, we see no practical means of doing more at this time than is already being done by the Government. The committee ask to be discharged from the further consideration of the petitions."[9]

While the first half of the nineteenth century saw numerous and continuous memorials and resolutions requesting federal assistance for various educational projects, such requests were presented only in terms of specific isolated local situations. No indication that the petitioners viewed their needs in terms of national policy is evident, nor is there any appearance before 1850 of consciously organized pressure. In 1850, however, the first small beginnings of such pressure were stirring, for in that year the legislature of the state of Michigan presented a petition to Congress for aid in furthering agricultural education. Although this petition was concerned only with aid for Michigan, and not with the establishment of national policy, it is significant as being among the first of a long series of resolutions from state legislatures regarding aid for education. Increasingly, the manifestations of local interest as evidenced by the pronouncements of state legislatures became powerful factors in the conduct of debates on the question of federal aid.

In 1852, the Massachusetts legislature forwarded a recommendation that Congress establish a national agricultural college, after the fashion of West Point. But probably most noteworthy, particularly in view of its ultimate adoption in principle, was the series of resolutions set forth by the legislature of Illinois in

[8]Richardson, *op. cit.*, V, 543 ff.
[9]*Congressional Globe*, 39 : 1, 3649.

1853. First to recognize local needs as part of a national concern, these resolutions requested public land grants for *each* state "for the more liberal and practical education of our industrial classes and their teachers." These resolutions were stimulated by the efforts of a professor in the state university, Jonathan B. Turner, and apparently attracted considerable national attention.[10]

REVIEW OF THE PROPOSALS AND GRANTS FOR FEDERAL AID TO EDUCATION PRIOR TO 1870

A survey of the early proposals and grants for federal aid to education can be logically divided into two basic types. First and most important was the series of grants which were made specifically for educational purposes. Less significant, but of considerable prominence in establishing precedents for federal aid, were various miscellaneous grants which came to be used wholly or partially in support of education by the states. As the preceding paragraphs have implied, most of these measures were not enacted in response to public pressure. Rather they were the products of farsighted statesmanship or the results of what was considered sound political maneuvering.

In terms of their significance for American education, as well as chronologically, the two famous Ordinances of 1785 and 1787 must be listed first. The importance of the policies and principles established by these pre-Constitutional decrees cannot be overemphasized. The familiar credo contained in the Ordinance of 1787—"Religion, morality, and knowledge being necessary to good government and the happiness of mankind, schools and the means of education shall forever be encouraged"—and the provision of the Ordinance of 1785, which it followed and reinforced and which reserved to education the sixteenth section in every township carved out of the public domain, were basic elements in the development of the peculiarly American public school system. While it is maintained by some that these measures were considered primarily as means of attracting settlers

[10]Edmund J. James, *The Origin of the Land Grant Act of 1862 and Some Account of Its Author, Jonathan B. Turner*, 14 ff.

rather than as educational advances, the strength of the precedents for public education thereby established cannot be denied.[11]

Further support for these principles appeared at the time of the admission to the Union of the state of Ohio in 1802. By the procedure known as the "enabling act," Congress granted authority to the territories to draft and submit for Congressional approval state constitutions *before* final admission to the Union. With the Enabling Act for Ohio, definite educational provisions were required of each new state constitution; these provisions were, in effect, agreements by the prospective states to the conditions and limitations of the various federal grants, including those for the support of education. Thus, Ohio, by assenting to the conditions relative to land grants set forth in the Ordinance of 1785, began the practice of riveting this provision into state constitutions as well.

Again, in 1806, the admission of Tennessee offered opportunity for the further strengthening of these policies. In addition to making the usual provisions for land reservations for Tennessee itself, this became the occasion for insuring the application of the sixteenth section to education throughout the Louisiana Territory. With the admission of Oregon to territorial status in 1848, the practice of reserving *two* sections per township for education was instituted.

In addition to the general policy of reserving certain lands for education, Congress early made grants for specific educational institutions or endeavors. For example, in 1819, lands were granted to Connecticut, the income from which was to support a seminary for the instruction of the deaf and dumb, and in 1838, lands in Florida were awarded to a Dr. Henry Perrine to support studies in tropical botany.

Thus, by the time of the first important debates over the extent to which the Federal Government should aid or support education—the proposals of Representative Justin S. Morrill of Vermont for subsidization of colleges of "agriculture and the

---

[11]Henry C. Taylor, *The Educational Significance of the Early Federal Land Ordinances*, 115.

mechanic arts" in 1857 and 1862—a considerable body of precedent had been established. The picture is not complete, however, without note being made of the steadily growing tendency on the part of the individual states to apply other federal grants, the provisions of which were general, to the support of education.

As before, the Enabling Act of Ohio in 1802 is significant. By this legislation, five percent of the net proceeds of public land sales within the state was granted to the state for "internal improvements." This practice was continued and such proceeds, first by Illinois in 1818 and later by all newly admitted states, came to be devoted at least in part to education. From 1824, many such grants specifically listed education as one of the "internal improvements," and Cubberley notes that, after 1860, all states admitted to the Union received this five percent expressly for the support of their common school funds.[12] Another provision of the Ohio Enabling Act granted saline lands and their proceeds to the state for internal improvements; Cubberley estimates that in those states which received such grants, approximately seventy-five percent has been devoted to education.[13]

Another measure which served to enhance the legitimacy of the federal aid principle was that distributing the surplus revenue in the Treasury among the states in 1836. Such a procedure had been advocated by Jefferson in 1808 as a means of furthering various state activities, including education.[14] By the law of 1836, over $28,000,000 was returned to the states with no specific proscription as to its use, but much went to the support of public schools. Similarly, with the Preemption Act of 1841, by which lands were granted to certain states to be sold to finance internal improvements, states were enabled to further the practice of channeling federal money into their school systems. And finally, in 1849, the Federal Government began to grant lands to states as reimbursement for the expenses incurred in reclaiming

<hr />

[12]Cubberley, op. cit., 32.
[13]Ibid., 31.
[14]Ibid., 32.

swamplands. These, too, were usually added to the states' educational funds.

The Morrill Bill of 1857 is noteworthy as the first attempt to establish through Congressional action a *national* policy with regard to federal aid to education. It is also significant as producing the first indication of the alignment of party forces with regard to this principle. Representative Morrill of Vermont, a Republican, proposed in this bill that each state be granted 20,000 acres of public land (or its equivalent in scrip) for each of its members of Congress, and that the proceeds of the sale of such lands be devoted to the establishment of colleges of agriculture and mechanic arts. Morrill's arguments in its favor and those of the opposition accurately foreshadowed many of the arguments which have been advanced in all federal aid debates since that time. In brief, Morrill noted that too much public land was falling into private hands and being exploited, that there was a need for scientific agriculture and industrial training, that the existing colleges were primarily classical and pre-professional, and that regional inequalities in the ability to support education existed. The relative importance to Morrill of the educational benefits of his bill may be implied from his statement that the bill constitutes "something for cheap scientific education" and "something for . . . the better support of Christian churches and common schools."[15]

The arguments of the opposition were summarized by President Buchanan in his veto message previously noted. The bill's alleged unconstitutionality, its interference with states' rights, its prodigality with the public patrimony, and the feeling that if it were legitimate to aid agricultural education it became logical to aid any education—these and lesser points constituted the case of the opponents of federal aid. Kandel's thorough summary of this Congressional activity indicates that, while the bill had considerable support in both Houses, the Southern Congressmen were almost solidly opposed, and they were joined by the Western Democrats.[16] The narrow votes of passage

[15]I. L. Kandel, *Federal Aid for Vocational Education, A Report to the Carnegie Foundation for the Advancement of Teaching*, Bulletin No. 10, 6.
[16]Kandel, *op. cit.*, 6 ff.

forecast the improbability of re-passage over a certain Democratic veto.[17]

The Morrill bill was reintroduced in 1861 and passed by the Thirty-ninth Congress in 1862. Though substantially the same bill, its second consideration served to crystallize further the opposing positions regarding the relation of the Federal Government to education. The major changes from the earlier proposal were two: the acreage per Congressman allotted to each state was increased to 30,000 acres, and the curricular proscription was broadened to include military training. While the debate on this measure occupied small parts of five separate days in the Senate, it was passed without any debate in the House. At least two related factors were instrumental in effecting its cursory consideration and its rapid passage. Most important, of course, was the absence of Southern representation, which constituted the real strength of the opposition in 1858. The fact of war also caused many in Congress to consider this as a war measure, in view of its provision for military training, and so perhaps hastened its passage. The opposition in 1862 came from a group of Midwestern Senators who violently feared the "encroachments" of Eastern interests and Seaboard states which, lacking public lands, would receive land scrip entitling them to parts of the public domain. Some few considered such legislation "visionary" or "mischievous,"[18] while others doubted the wisdom of including military training, maintaining that it was "incongruous" with the aims of an agricultural or mechanic arts curriculum.[19] Outside the halls of Congress there was considerable opposition to the bill from private college interests which, if they could not monopolize, wanted to participate in the activities for which federal aid was being proposed,[20] but the debates in Congress indicate that this pressure was of small consequence.

[17]William B. Parker, *The Life and Public Services of Justin Smith Morrill*, 277.

[18]Matthew H. Buckham, address at the *Justin Smith Morrill Centenary Exercises Celebrated by the State of Vermont at Montpelier April Fourteenth*, 1910.

[19]Arthur C. Cole, *The Irrepressible Conflict: 1850-1865*, 370.

[20]James, *op. cit.*

These considerations led the opponents to reiterate the charges of unconstitutionality, invasion of states' rights, and the evils of federal control which had been mentioned four years before and which have continued to comprise the strongest and most appealing of arguments down to the present.

The educational significance of the Morrill Act is profound and has been repeatedly described elsewhere. It is interesting to note, however, that its passage was probably due far more to considerations of political strategy than to concern for the advancement of education. The Congressional debate, for example, made little mention of the educational provisions of the bill, except to declare education outside the federal purview. Very little thought seems to have been given, either by Representative Morrill or by others, to the actual program of study to be fostered. Taylor, in his study of *The Educational Significance of the Early Federal Land Ordinances*, writes: "The fact that the schools thus founded were vocational and of especial value to a definite and powerful class of voters is of political rather than of educational significance. Without doubt, the motives behind this legislation grew out of political necessity rather than educational interest. Nevertheless, it is important to note that it was thought that political necessity could best be served by liberal land grants for a form of higher education."[21] Wellington states that "with the growth of sections having conflicting economic interests the disposition of the public lands became a subject for sectional alliances and political bargaining."[22] Thus Kandel seems to conclude that Morrill and the Republican party were primarily anxious to ingratiate themselves with the farmers in such a way as to allow the continued maintenance of a higher tariff structure for the benefit of Eastern manufacturers.[23] As late as 1879, F. A. P. Barnard expressed himself as unsure of the wisdom of the Morrill Act. He felt that ". . . the considerations which induced this legislation were not probably those large and liberal ones I have above suggested—considerations which should logi-

[21]Taylor, *op. cit.*, 121.
[22]Quoted in Kandel, *op. cit.*, 86.
[23]*Ibid.*

cally lead to the endowment just as freely of schools for lawyers and engineers as of schools for mechanics and farmers—but the fact that there are, as politicians are quite well aware, a great many mechanics and a great many farmers in the country, and not by any means as many engineers or lawyers."[24]

Thus out of political as well as educational consideration came legislation of immense benefit to public education. As a precedent for national participation in educational affairs, the Morrill Act ranks in importance second only to the Ordinances of 1785 and 1787. While its place as a landmark in the development of a policy of federal support for education is adequately recognized, the Morrill Act is perhaps not so well known for the contributions it made to the techniques of implementing that policy. It was the first enactment of national policy to grant federal support for specifically prescribed educational purposes—the promotion of "the liberal and practical education of the industrial classes in the several pursuits and professions of life"—and to indicate the type of institution to be supported. It should be noted that opponents of federal aid have consistently pointed to this feature as dictating the curricula, hence invading local prerogatives. Perhaps more significant in the long run was the system provided by the Morrill Act whereby lands were taken from those states which possessed them and were made available to those states which had none. Theoretically, then, here was a formula designed in a sense to equalize educational opportunity, though subsequent misuse and abuse of the lands so obtained impeded the fulfillment of this aspect of the scheme. Nevertheless, in view of the contemporary essentiality of making education equally available to all, here perhaps is a parallel of importance. Are not current proposals suggesting that federal moneys be similarly distributed, on the basis of a progressive formula of taking the money from the places where it is and applying it for the benefit of those who have none?

The picture of the influence on precedent of the Morrill Act is not complete without a glance at the debate which was occasioned by a proposal to amend the act in 1864. Then, when a

[24]F. A. P. Barnard, *Education and the State*, 10.

measure extending the time limit within which states could qualify for the benefits of the act was under consideration, an amendment was suggested whereby the states could elect to apply their lands to the colleges of agriculture and mechanic arts *or* to sundry other purposes, notably the provision of common school education for war orphans. Sponsored by Representative Holman of Kansas, a leading opponent of the landgrant principle, this was an amendment of desperation designed to cripple the basic intent of the original act. The remarks occasioned by this proposal are worthy of note, however. Representative Holman maintained that "The appropriation of these lands to an agricultural college is a measure of partial benefit; a handful of citizens, presidents, and professors, a small number of favored youths already possessed of the benefits of commonschool education, with parents able to educate them, will always derive any benefit such institutions can furnish. The State should have nothing to do with colleges designed to benefit favored classes of its people."[25] Therefore, said Holman, let the individual states decide how they shall make use of these lands. To the defense of the original purpose of the act came Representative Morrill: "The object of the original donation was to enable the industrial classes of the country to obtain a cheap, solid, and substantial education. I trust the House will not begin thus early to fritter away the whole purpose of that act."—Representative Thaddeus Stevens of Pennsylvania: "When the original bill was framed it was intended to be national and to establish a national system of education, bestowing national property for that purpose, and anything that would mar the harmony of that great measure I think ought to be discouraged by this House."—and Representative Clay of Kentucky: The proposed amendments "are destructive of the whole bill. If any particular State is allowed to do what it pleases with this land, then all the States will come here for the same privilege."[26] The defeat of the amendment insured the continuation of a limited but definite degree of federal control over state educational

[25]*Congressional Globe*, 38 : 1, 1284.
[26]*Ibid.*

activity. While heretofore fears had been expressed over the evils of such control, it was with this debate upon the extension of the Morrill Act that Congress first came to grips with that issue. Bit by bit the body of precedent was enlarged.

OTHER NATIONAL EDUCATIONAL LEGISLATION PRIOR TO *1870*

The background for the federal aid struggles from 1870 to 1890 is not finally established without consideration of two additional national educational efforts. Though neither the educational activity of the Freedmen's Bureau nor the establishment of a Federal Department of Education was a strictly federal aid measure, the enactment and the experience of each by 1870 played no small part in conditioning the developing attitudes of educators and Congressmen.

The Bureau of Refugees, Freedmen, and Abandoned Lands (commonly called the Freedmen's Bureau) was established by act of Congress in March, 1865. It was unquestionably a war measure, an act of military necessity. As Northern armies brought more and more Confederate territory under federal control, the problem of caring for the newly emancipated Negro grew ever larger. It was early recognized that food, clothing, and employment were the urgent requirements, but the desirability of moral and intellectual education was not overlooked.[27] Various agencies had begun to assume charge of the Negro problem as early as 1862: the Army, the Treasury Department, and several churches and benevolent societies. Each of these attempted to provide some educational facilities; but while the Army had the authority to establish and operate schools—and occasionally did so with success—as in New Orleans under General Banks[28]—most of the work of education was left to the benevolent and religious organizations. Thus it was that the Secretary of War's report (1863) on the matter of care of the freedmen provided for "secular and religious schools supported

[27]Paul S. Peirce, *The Freedmen's Bureau: A Chapter in the History of Reconstruction*, 2.
[28]Peirce, *op. cit.*, 20.

largely by benevolent societies."[29] This plan, in effect, became the core of the rather meager educational activities of the Freedmen's Bureau.

The first legislative proposal for such a bureau was presented by Representative Thomas Eliot of Massachusetts in January, 1863, but its consideration was not obtained until February, 1864. In his remarks regarding the advisability of establishing the agency, Eliot did include education of the Negro as one of the Federal Government's responsibilities, but that it was definitely subordinate was indicated by the presence of only two very brief references to education in a lengthy address to the House. The bill creating the Freedmen's Bureau, which was passed despite considerable disapproval, made no provision for appropriations for schools.[30] It was not until the second Freedmen's Bureau Act of July, 1866 that definite concern for education was evidenced. This act greatly enlarged the educational authority of the Bureau, by sanctioning official cooperation in educational activity with the benevolent societies and by appropriating $521,000 to defray certain school expenses. The Bureau was empowered to rent or otherwise acquire buildings for schools, however, only when "teachers and means of instruction without cost to the government should be provided," presumably by the charitable organizations.[31]

Reports of the operations of the Bureau indicate that the major financial support for Negro education continued to come from the benevolent societies. The Bureau apparently was primarily concerned with stimulating private donations and spurring state or local governments to set up and maintain their own school systems. General O. O. Howard, the Commissioner of the Bureau, considered the function of his office to be that of affording "unity and system" to the education of the freedmen—i.e. the exercise of control without the burden of support.[32] Peirce has analyzed the expenditures of the Bureau for educa-

29*Ibid.*, 12.
30*Ibid.*, 43-44.
31*Ibid.*, 76.
32O. O. Howard, *Report of the Commissioner of the Bureau of Refugees, Freedmen, and Abandoned Lands* (1866), 9-10.

tion and finds that the annual outlays rose from $27,000 in 1865
to $1,000,000 in 1870 and that the total for education from
1865 through 1871 equaled $5,262,511. This represents more
than half the money spent for schools under the supervision of
the Freedmen's Bureau, the rest being borne by private associations. But the gradual and continued increase of educational
activity among the Negroes supported wholly by private bene-
faction or local taxes meant that at no time was the Federal
Government bearing half the total burden.[33]

Thus the significance of the Freedmen's Bureau as a precursor of the later federal aid struggles lies more in what it did
not do than in what it accomplished. Its basic reliance upon private and local support of educational effort and the fact that it
was concerned only with one segment of the population suggest the question as to whether or not it should rightly be considered a measure of federal aid in the sense that the term has
come to imply. Nevertheless, the mere fact of federal participation, however limited, in local educational endeavor undoubtedly had an effect upon the protagonists and the opponents of further federal activity. Some were to say that the
Bureau's work was merely the beginning of recognition of federal responsibility, while others would point to it as a military
measure devoid of any status as precedent; and yet others would
find this, as they had found earlier acts, an unconstitutional
procedure.

Considerably more important, in terms of both its influence
on long-range educational developments and its effect upon
immediate post-Civil War thinking, was the establishment in
March, 1867 of a Federal Department of Education. Section One
of the organic act set forth the purpose of the legislation in these
words: "That there shall be established . . . a department of education for the purpose of collecting such statistics and facts as
shall show the condition and progress of education in the several
states and territories, and of diffusing such information" relative to school administration, methodology, etc. as shall "promote the cause of education throughout the country." Of the

[33]Peirce, op. cit., 82.

actual duties of the new office, Section Three required the Commissioner of Education, appointed by the President to serve under the Secretary of the Interior, to make annual reports to Congress as to the findings of his department and his recommendations for more effective fulfillment of "the purpose for which this department is established."[34] It is apparent that, as originally instituted, this "department" was designed to operate merely as an agency for the collection and publication of educational data. Neither its status nor its budget allowed a semblance of power or prestige. And yet, despite the skepticism and hostility attendant upon its creation, this was a notable event in the history of federal relations to education. In order accurately to evaluate its influence upon subsequent developments, it is necessary to examine briefly the expressions of public sentiment and the Congressional activity which preceded and surrounded its establishment.

The earliest efforts to interest the Federal Government in the collection, analysis, and diffusion of data concerning education were made by Henry Barnard in 1837. As a direct result of his agitations, the census of 1840, by incorporating certain statistics relative to illiteracy and educational activities, became the first federal operation of this kind.[35] Gradually, the benefits of such services came to be recognized by many educators with the result that, in 1849, the teachers of Essex County, Massachusetts, petitioned Congress for the establishment of a "bureau in the home department for promoting public education."[36] In the same year, a New England group calling itself the "friends of the common schools" urged Congress to establish a national office to collect and publish educational statistics.[37] The American Institute of Instruction, which Judd considers the earliest important teachers' association, after studying the proposals of Henry Barnard for such an agency, in 1851 began a campaign

---

[34] Darrell H. Smith, *The Bureau of Education; Its History, Activities, and Organization*, 2-3.

[35] *Ibid.*, 1.

[36] Richard G. Boone, *Education in the United States: Its History from the Earliest Settlements*, 309.

[37] Robert H. Mahoney, *The Federal Government and Education*, 8.

of memorializing Congress in its behalf,[38] as did the Association for the Advancement of Education from 1854,[39] the National Teachers' Association (the forerunner of the modern National Education Association) continuously from 1859,[40] and various state educational organizations. These were the beginnings of organized professional efforts to obtain federal assistance in the provision of public education.

The spark was struck, however, by the address of E. E. White, Commissioner of Common Schools for Ohio, before the National Association of State and City School Superintendents on February 7, 1866. Laying down the premise that republican democracy requires universal education, White inquired into the function of the general (i.e. federal) government. He noted that three approaches to the question were then current. The first, a federally established and maintained system of education, he rejected as placing the control of education too far from the people. The second, Congressional enforcement of the maintenance of adequate schools in each state, he found desirable only in a time of crisis. The third alternative, the establishment of a national agency to encourage and "induce each state to maintain an efficient school system," he considered not only desirable but essential.[41] This address, according to Shiras, led the superintendents' association (perhaps the most influential group of educators of that period) to memorialize Congress in the strongest terms in favor of a national bureau for educational affairs.[42] And it was this memorial which Representative James A. Garfield of Ohio presented when he introduced, on February 18, 1866, a bill to establish a "Department of Education."

While the proponents of the bureau repeatedly voiced their aversion to federal control of education, except for a few who demanded federal responsibility for the education of the Negro,

[38]Charles H. Judd, *Research in the United States Office of Education*, 1.
[39]*Ibid.*
[40]William T. Harris, "Establishment of the Office of the Commissioner of Education of the United States and Henry Barnard's Relation to It," *Report of the Commissioner of Education for the Year 1902*, I, 906.
[41]E. E. White, "National Bureau of Education," *American Journal of Education*, XVI, 180.
[42]Alex Shiras, *The National Bureau of Education*, 2.

there were those who saw in the proposal new encroachments on local and state prerogatives.[43] These were in the minority, however, and were primarily expressions of opinion from New England, where many felt that the public schools were entirely adequate and required no outside assistance.

The interest of the press, both lay and professional, in the projected federal agency was minimal. Of the educational journals, the *American Education Monthly*, the official organ of certain state teachers' associations and the most widely circulated periodical of its class at the time,[44] expressed the most concern. In advocating the bureau, it went far beyond the provisions of the Garfield bill in recommending the areas of federal responsibility.[45] Daily newspaper coverage was meager at best. Of the New York journals, only the *Times* definitely committed itself to the purposes of the bill,[46] while the *Tribune* took occasion to indulge in sarcasm: "The House will have the unanimous approbation of the country in every effort to enlighten the capital."[47] Newspapers outside the New York area gave no evidence of awareness of the pending legislation.

Legislative activity leading to the establishment of the bureau began in December, 1865 with the adoption of a resolution submitted by Representative Ignatius Donnelly of Minnesota, which called upon the joint committee on reconstruction to "inquire into the expediency of establishing in the capital a National Bureau of Education." Donnelly viewed the bureau as one with power to enforce minimum standards of education on all states and as an "essential and permanent part of any system of reconstruction."[48] After the introduction of the bill by Garfield, in June, 1866, it received the support of several eminent Republicans, some of whom, like Donnelly, considered the functions of the proposed agency to be much more far-reaching than either the professional educators or the Congressional

---

43*The Massachusetts Teacher*, XIX, 13.

44Frank Luther Mott, *A History of American Magazines*, III, 167.

45*American Education Monthly*, March, 1865, 86-87, and July, 1866, 270-271.

46New York *Times*, June 9, 1866, 4, and March 2, 1867, 4.

47New York *Tribune*, June 9, 1866, 4.

48*Congressional Globe*, 39 : 1, 60.

sponsors had contemplated. Representatives George Boutwell of Massachusetts and Garfield, both strong supporters of the measure, were forced to deny unequivocally the extremes of federal power which some were attempting to read into the bill. Garfield, whose "ceaseless efforts" in private in behalf of the bill were credited as largely responsible for its final passage,[49] stated during the debate: "The genius of our Government does not allow us to establish a compulsory system of education, as is done in some of the countries of Europe. . . . It is for each state to decide."[50]

In both House and Senate, opposition to the proposed bureau was strong and vocal. George F. Hoar, then Representative from Massachusetts, noted in his *Autobiography*, that "The office was exceedingly unpopular, not only with the Old Democrats and the Strict Constructionists, who insisted on leaving such things to the States, but with a large class of Republicans."[51] Typical of the reactions of this last group is this statement from the remarks in debate of Representative Pike of Maine, who predicted that "The school-houses of the country will go under the control of the General Government. Churches, I suppose, are to follow next. So, taking the railroads, telegraphs, school-houses, and churches, it would seem Congress would leave little to us but our local taxation and our local pauperism."[52]

The vote on the Department of Education bill took place too soon after the Civil War to permit any conclusive comparison of the two major parties with regard to their stands on this issue. Ex-Confederate states, hence the Democratic party, had not yet been restored to their peacetime Congressional status, thus the disagreements here were primarily within the Republican party. The vote on final passage in the House (no vote was recorded in the Senate) indicates rather marked Republican solidarity on the question of federal participation in education—72 Republicans in favor, 16 in opposition—while the reverse is

[49]Burke A. Hinsdale, "Documents Illustrative of American Educational History," *Report of the U. S. Commissioner of Education* for 1892-1893, 1289.
[50]Shiras, *op. cit.,* 10.
[51]George F. Hoar, *Autobiography of Seventy Years,* 264.
[52]*Congressional Globe,* 39 : 1, 3047.

true for the Democratic forces—3 in favor, 25 opposed. The Republican opponents were largely from the Midwest and New England, as were the Democratic proponents, but no strictly geographical alignment is discernible in the over-all vote picture. In the only manifestation of Senatorial sentiment, a vote on a motion to reconsider the previous passage of the bill, a similar alignment can be noted. The bill was signed by President Johnson on March 2, 1867, only after he had received definite assurances that no centralization of educational activity was envisioned.[53] Hostility to the new agency did not die, however, and in 1868 strong attempts to effect its abolition resulted in an amendment which, while leaving its functions unchanged, greatly lowered its prestige and its budget. The "Department" became the Bureau of Education, it was placed under the supervision of the Secretary of the Interior, and its staff and salaries were reduced.

Despite these rather inauspicious beginnings, the creation of a federal agency concerned with public education and the debate attendant thereon occupies a prominent place in any survey of the development of federal aid to education. In the first place, this action served to crystallize the sentiments of legislators, and to some extent of educators, relative to this question. The National Education Association felt constrained to register the following expression of opinion in 1869: "Resolved that in petitioning Congress for the creation of a Department of Education in connection with General Government, this association contemplates neither the establishment of a national system of education nor any interference whatsoever with the systems of education established in the several states."[54] And the educational organization of Virginia noted that the national bureau of education "deserves liberal support as long as its duties are confined to its present useful work of collecting, systematizing, and distributing educational information. . . . But we fear that there are men in Congress who would like to erect this department

[53]Bernard C. Steiner, *Life of Henry Barnard*, Department of the Interior, Bureau of Education, Bulletin 1919, No. 8, 108.
[54]Shiras, *op. cit.*, 9.

into a central authority with compulsory powers."[55] Many years later, the *American Catholic Quarterly* commented: "But in time it became evident that the Bureau of Education was part of a scheme to bring the whole school system of the separate States under the control of Congress."[56]

It must be noted in the second place, however, that this legislation, despite the controversy it inaugurated, resulted in more adequate recognition of the place of education as a *national* concern than had heretofore been the case. One cannot overlook the fact that within two years after the passage of this act both houses of Congress had established committees to deal specifically with educational matters. The importance of this development can hardly be overestimated.

SUMMARY

When, in 1871, the struggle to obtain federal support for common school education began, to what in precedent and experience could the American people and their legislators look for guidance?

1. While the Constitution makes no specific mention of federal responsibility for educational activity, fundamental commitments to the principle had actually antedated the adoption of the Constitution, i.e. the Ordinances of 1785 and 1787, and many of the "founding fathers" had subscribed to its further implementation.

2. Presidents, Congressmen, and other leaders had repeatedly expressed their belief in the desirability of federal aid to education, but a strong body of agreement in opposition from equally important sources had also developed.

3. After 1850, public interest in federal aid and pressure to obtain it had increasingly recognized the need for a *national* policy.

4. A long and steady series of federal enactments, from the Ordinance of 1785 to the Morrill Act of 1862, had established

[55]"The National Bureau of Education," *Educational Journal of Virginia,* 1871, 119.

[56]*American Catholic Quarterly,* 1888, 346.

legislative precedents upon which further national support could be based.

5. Over the same period, the states had gradually institution-alized the practice of applying various general federal grants to the support of public education.

6. The Morrill Act of 1862 had marked the first Congression-al commitment to a national policy of support for specific types of educational activity. Its passage had occasioned official expres-sions of belief in a certain degree of federal control over local educational efforts and had indicated the beginnings of the ap-plication of a progressive technique for the equalization of edu-cational opportunity.

7. Organized pressure for federal participation in education had begun to appear in connection with attempts to obtain a federal Department or Bureau of Education.

8. The debates on the Morrill Act and the establishment of a federal Department of Education had served to crystallize the opposing positions with regard to federal aid to education.

· III ·

THE ATTEMPT TO ESTABLISH A NATIONAL SYSTEM OF EDUCATION: 1870-1871

THE CONDITION OF EDUCATION IN THE SOUTH
1870-1880

ANY legislation is proposed out of a complex of contributory conditions, not the least of which are economic. The attempts to enact federal aid legislation during the 1870's and 1880's were intimately related to the condition of education and the general economic situation. As all of these proposals were directed primarily at lessening critical conditions in the South, it is well, before attempting to analyze the bills themselves and the pressures which surrounded them, to present a brief description of the Southern economy and the educational situation it produced.

Economic Conditions in the South

The economic conditions of the post-Civil War South have been adequately described elsewhere and detailed repetition is not required here. The war and the period of reconstruction which followed prostrated the South, and it is perhaps not inappropriate to describe the situation as one in which the only direction the economy could move was upward—in the direction of greater production. While new circumstances—emancipation of the Negro in particular—outmoded the old paternalistic plantation pattern, they "did not essentially alter the previous system of huge estates operated by servile labor, interspersed with numerous holdings of yeoman farmers and with the run-down or never valuable tracts of small freeholders and tenants. . . . The

supposed breakup of the plantation system was in part a trans-
ference from gang labor to tenancy."[1] While many authorities
point to this period as one in which the number of farms increased markedly, Shannon accounts for this by noting that
farm tenancy and share-cropping "mounted alarmingly" and
indicates that such holdings were counted as "farm" in any agricultural census.[2] Nevertheless, the first area to begin to re-
establish itself was that of agriculture. Despite adherence to a
crop-lien system of credit and the enforcement of one-crop cul-
tivation, the gradual introduction of new methods of agriculture and diverse crops was a feature of the period here under
investigation. Slowly but steadily crops grew in size and value.

Industrial development, too, was characteristic of this period
in Southern history. From 1880 to 1890 "the number of spindles
and looms almost trebled. . . . The manufacture of iron, equally
favored by natural conditions, made as notable progress. . . .
During the eighties, fifty new blast furnaces were erected in
Alabama, Tennessee, and Virginia."[3] Other new industries by
the score sprang up throughout the South and a remarkable expansion of railroad mileage was effected. As with the rest of the
United States, the panic of 1873 and the less acute depression of
1884-1885 temporarily retarded but did not stop these advances.

What did this economic progress mean in terms of the resources available for school support? Here the picture is not so
favorable. For example, in the late 1880's, when many were
maintaining that the South had reached a point at which it could
easily support its own schools, the Commissioner of Education
reported that in the Northern and Western states $2,225 per
child in taxable wealth existed, while in the South the wealth per
child equaled $851. [4] The assessed valuation per capita by re-

[1]Fred A. Shannon, *The Farmers' Last Frontier: Agriculture 1860-1897*, 76.
[2]*Ibid.*, 81.
[3]Arthur M. Schlesinger, *Political and Social Growth of the United States:
1852-1933*, 145.
[4]*Report of the Commissioner of Education for the Year 1887-88*, 22 ff.
Such data as are here presented, derived primarily from the censuses of 1870
and 1880, cannot be considered as accurate, in view of inadequate census
techniques and unreliable appraisals of property values. They are useful, however, as suggesting the general economic situation in relation to the problem
of school support.

gions was listed as follows: for New England—$661, for the West—$334, for the Middle Atlantic States—$473, for the territories—$337, and for the South—$155.[5] In general, despite the rapid and spectacular industrial and agricultural developments of the post-Civil War years, the assessed valuation of most Southern states dropped drastically, while at the same time the populations were markedly increasing.[6]

Educational Conditions in the South

The census figures of 1870 and 1880 indicate an increase in the population of the United States during the decade from 38,558,371 to 50,155,783. The number of Negroes, most of whom continued to live in the South, increased from four million in 1860 to approximately six million in 1880. The educational problem is starkly portrayed by the data which describe (1) the ratio of child population to adult population and (2) the extent of illiteracy.

In 1870, for every 1,000 adults in Arkansas, there were 1,409 minors—this represents the most acute expression of this discrepancy in the country; while in Louisiana, relatively the most favored Southern state in this respect, for every 1,000 adults there were 1,109 persons under 21 years of age. This compares with a Northern situation in which Indiana's ratio was 1,234 minors for each 1,000 adults, while New Hampshire held only 675 minors for each 1,000 adults.[7] By 1880, the acuteness of this condition had been relieved somewhat, but the ratio of persons under 21 years of age to adults in the South still stood at 1,242 for every 1,000, whereas in the North that relationship was 909 minors for every 1,000 adults.[8]

---

[5]Henry W. Blair, *The Education Bill*, 38. Of this compilation prepared by the Bureau of Education and based on the 10th Census (1880), Blair wrote: "These tables represent an indescribable amount of my personal work and weariness, and I may overestimate their importance; but ... the educational condition of no people was ever so well delineated statistically" as in this presentation.

[6]*Ibid.*, 35.

[7]Charles Warren, *Illiteracy in the United States in 1870 and 1880, with Diagnosis and Observations*, 13-14.

[8]Commissioner of Education, *op. cit.*, 29.

A similar, yet more sharply differentiated, picture is presented by the data relative to illiteracy. (Illiteracy is here defined, as it was by the Bureau of the Census and the Bureau of Education when these data were compiled, as the inability to write.) The Ninth Census (1870) reported the state of illiteracy in the United States as follows.[9] Of the total number of illiterates— 5,660,074:

	North	South	Pacific
White—2,879,543	1,262,113	1,516,339	101,091
Colored—2,763,991	91,092	2,671,396	1,503

Of the population of the Northern states, 7.7 percent were found illiterate, for the Pacific states the percentage stood at 15 percent, while for the Southern region (this included the old slave states plus West Virginia and the District of Columbia) the population was found to be 42.1 percent illiterate.[10] It should be noted finally that, while in the North 93 percent of the illiteracy was among the white population, in the South only 36 percent of the illiteracy was present among whites, the remaining 64 percent existing among the Negro population. Warren found that by 1880 the percentage of illiteracy in the South had diminished by about five percent over 1870, but the absolute number of illiterates had increased by over half a million. This increase occurred in all of the Southern states with the exception of Delaware. Of this increase, over two-thirds was among the colored population.[11]

After the Civil War, increased private benefactions and prodigious local efforts in the South had produced remarkable advances in education. Thus, the South, with over five million children of school age, was able to raise approximately $10,000,000 per year for school support in the late 1870's. At the same time, however, the Northern section, with twice as many children to care for, raised *six* times as much to finance its schools.[12] Many were to answer this with the rejoinder that if the South wished

[9]*Ibid.,* 64.

[10]Warren, *op. cit.,* 71.

[11]*Ibid.,* 17.

[12]Dexter A. Hawkins, "National Aid to State Common School Education," *Bureau of Education Circular of Information No. 2,* 1882, 52.

better educational facilities, it had only to demonstrate the willingness to support education that was typical of the Northern communities by increasing taxes. Blair's tabulations indicate that, in view of the condition of the region, the South was doing far more in this respect already than were the other sections. His data show that the South was spending a larger percentage of state and local taxes upon education than were the Middle Atlantic states in 1880, and only a small fraction of a percentage point less than even the New England states.[13] Even with such efforts, however, analysis of the condition of the facilities thus provided in the South shows the extent of their inadequacies. At best, the Southern school year lasted only four months in the 1880's, teachers' salaries were phenomenally low (Knight states that from 1860 to 1900 the average annual teacher's salary in the South dropped from $175 to $159, while in 1900 the average for the nation as a whole was $310),[14] and though improving enrollment records could be presented, the increases in actual school attendance were not keeping pace with the growth of the school age population.[15] It was this condition which was causing many persons, both North and South, to question the sufficiency of local and private resources alone.

It remains only to canvass briefly the evidence of Southern advance in the late 1880's, for it was after 1886 that the campaign for federal aid rapidly lost its momentum in the face (among other factors) of vehement assertions of Southern readiness and ability to help itself. As will be noted later, the critical year was 1886-1887, for it was in this year that those proclaiming Southern prosperity began to make themselves heard. It was true that in 1888 the South could point to the enrollment of a larger percentage of its *total* population than could the North, but this constituted a smaller percentage of the school-age pop-

[13]Blair, *op. cit.,* 39-40.
[14]Edgar W. Knight, *Public Education in the South,* 422.
[15]It should be noted that these data, and the sources from which they are derived, are such that the proportion of white to colored children and indications of the extent of the effort for Negro education are not obtainable. In many instances the reports rendered to the Bureau of Education by the states did not include Negro children in their figures.

ulation of the South.[16] It was also true that critics of federal aid could cite Southern cities and towns in which the school facilities compared favorably with those of the North, but as the Superintendent of Schools for Georgia noted in 1889, the common school problem of the South was primarily a rural problem. Of Georgia's 560,281 school-age children in that year, 490,270 were inhabitants of rural areas. This "is the case of the South" as a whole.[17] Coupled with this situation, of course, was the fact that whatever prosperity had developed was concentrated in the cities while, in general, the rural areas remained in as dire need as before. Nor should it be forgotten that the group which was in greatest need of educational assistance—the Negroes—was the group least able to contribute anything approximating an equitable portion of any school fund.

Knight has summarized this period of Southern educational development and concludes that, while the spirit and the willingness to foster education may have been characteristic of the region during these years, it was only after the turn of the century—*not* in the middle of the 1880's—that the economy was sufficiently healthy to permit more adequate school support. He writes of the period 1876 to 1890: "Heroic efforts at readjustment were made during those years, but the schools did not respond to the needs of the period, and educational improvement was very slow except in those towns and cities which had received assistance from the Peabody Fund. . . . And even in those communities the growth of public education was not particularly marked, though the proof of their interest in schools was the gradual increase in their willingness to vote local taxes for public educational support. Outside the larger towns and cities, however, the condition of public schools was generally deplorable."[18] Knight goes on to note that economic recovery was very slow until 1890, but that between 1890 and 1900 the wealth of the South increased by 50 percent. "This became the basis of substantial increases in school revenues and the foun-

16Arthur M. Schlesinger, *The Rise of the City: 1878-1898*, 165.

17Atticus G. Haygood, "The South and the School Problem," *Harpers'*, 79:226, July, 1889.

18Knight, *op. cit.*, 415-416.

dation of a new attitude toward education which began to make itself felt throughout the South after 1900."[19]

PUBLIC PRESSURE WITH REGARD TO FEDERAL AID TO EDUCATION

In order to analyze and assess adequately the public sentiment existing in 1870 which might be said to have led to the proposal of a national system of education (the Hoar bill), it is necessary to consider first the evidences of public opinion regarding the more general issue of federal participation in education. While there was some pressure directly favoring such a system, there was considerably more of a demand for a still unelaborated federal "assistance" to education, and it would be incorrect to assume that all who wished federal aid were in sympathy with such a proposal. It becomes increasingly evident, as one studies the manifestations of these pressures—petitions to Congress, newspaper and magazine editorials, statements of individuals, and the like—that by 1870-1871, no clearcut conception of the form federal aid should take had crystallized in the minds of either the professional educators or the general public. But it was in direct response to the educational needs of this period that the first concrete pressures for federal aid appeared, and it was here that national legislative proposals to meet such an educational situation first received any serious consideration from the press.

Concern for the matter of federal participation in education did not arise overnight. Its roots have been traced briefly in Chapter II. But concern for the relationship of the Federal Government to the operations of local common schools could show in 1870 only a short history. One of the earliest statements in this area appeared as the lead editorial in the opening issue of the *American Educational Monthly*, in January, 1864. Though not yet the influential journal it was soon to become, this periodical chose to emphasize at its birth the growing need for concern for education as a national as well as a local problem,

[19]*Ibid.*, 425.

noting that upon the "faithful accomplishment [of education] depends the highest success of all the other functions" of the national government.[20] Subsequent issues of this monthly demonstrated that here had been launched a notable and powerful campaign against the dogmatic worship of states' rights in educational affairs.

While it was not a plea for federal participation, a statement by the New York *Tribune* in 1866 which commented upon the formation of a Committee on Education in the national House of Representatives bears noting. The editors wrote that "The committee contains one member from New England, the home of the Common School System. The day that shall see that system rooted in the Southern States will see the end of all serious perils to the security and integrity of the Union."[21] There was growing among many who gave thought to these matters a conviction that national political unity and strength were largely dependent upon and conditioned by an effective education, and particularly by a sound "common school" education. It was but a short step to a feeling that the national government had a responsibility for the nurturing and improvement of the educational system. Thus it was not unnatural that, in 1868, the National Labor Union resolved, in the words of Terence V. Powderley, that "it is the imperative duty of Congress to make such wise and just regulations as shall afford all the means of acquiring knowledge requisite to the intelligent exercise of the privileges and duties pertaining to sovereignty."[22]

Of organized pressure for federal participation in education there was as yet little. Logically, it was the professional educational associations which first exerted efforts in this direction. Again it was the National Association of School Superintendents which led the way. Memorializing Congress in 1870, the association maintained that no sound program of reconstruction could ignore the need for a "general system of education"

[20]"National Education," *American Educational Monthly*, 1:19-20, January, 1864.
[21]New York *Tribune*, February 15, 1866, 4.
[22]Philip R. V. Curoe, *Educational Attitudes and Policies of Organized Labor in the United States*, 74.

throughout the country. It urged upon the Federal Government the responsibility of equalizing the educational funds of the states and hoped for the continuation of the work inaugurated by the Freedmen's Bureau.[23] But it was General John Eaton, the second Commissioner of Education, who in 1870 expressed most forcefully the prevailing sentiment of those in the profession who favored such activity by the Federal Government. Succeeding Henry Barnard to an office which was undergoing severe criticism, which many were attempting to abolish, and which many people at that time wanted to see continued only as a mere data-collecting agency, Eaton immediately gave voice to his belief in a policy of action for the Federal Government in support of education. In an address to the National Teachers' Association in 1870, Eaton presented his conception of the responsibilities of the national government in educational affairs. In brief, he asserted that:

1. The national government is responsible for education in the territories and in the District of Columbia, and for the education of the Indians.

2. The national government "may do all that its international relations require in regard to education."

3. The national government has the right to call the states or localities to account for their use of the federal grants-in-aid, and it may use either lands or money to administer such aid.

4. The national government is responsible for collecting, analyzing, and publicizing information about education throughout the country.

5. The national government "may make laws for these several purposes . . . (such laws require) a national educational office and officer. . . ."

6. "The national government should take no action calculated to decrease local or individual effort for education."

7. "The national government . . . may not suffer either the local or general prevalence of ignorance, that shall result in

[23]*Proceedings of the National Association of School Superintendents*, March, 1870, 12-13.

the destruction of the principles of liberty by the centralization of power."[24]

Most prominent after the educational profession in voicing opinions on this subject was the Catholic Church. Noting that, as the interest in and the demands for some sort of federal educational policy mounted, increasing attention was directed toward the relation of such activity to parochial education, the Church early presented its case. The Catholic position as it appeared in various statements in the year 1869, for example, was substantially as follows. "We are not hostile to the public schools, but, on the contrary, most earnestly anxious to secure for them the widest usefulness and the greatest efficiency." However, in maintaining that all education must take place in a "Christian atmosphere," Catholic spokesmen were unable to approve of schools and classes where divergent faiths and their various interpretations of history and society would be indiscriminately mixed. Thus, while expressing sympathy for the common school system, they found themselves unable to make use of that system, though willing to contribute to its support. As the issue of federal participation in or assistance to public education loomed larger, Catholics began to ask that they "be allowed to participate in the only way open to them, that is, by the apportionment of a ratable part of the fund, in aid of their . . . schools . . . subject to the limited supervision of the State. . . ."[25] Three points are significant in these statements. The first is that the Catholic leadership was aware of the probable trends in federal aid legislation (note the reference to an educational "fund" to be distributed) well before any such proposals were made to Congress, and, to judge by their pronouncements and memorials, much earlier than any other group. Second, there is here a definite concern that the Federal Government operate in a "limited" capacity, an expression of latent

---

[24]John Eaton, *The Relation of the National Government to Public Education*, 7-10; Darrell H. Smith, *The Bureau of Education: Its History, Activities, and Organizations*, 11.

[25]"The Catholic View of Public Education in the United States," *American Educational Monthly*, 6:1-13, January, 1869; "The Educational Question," *Catholic World*, 9:130, April, 1869.

fear that such legislation might lead to far greater federal authority over education than the Church could condone. And third, there is a marked identity between these early Catholic statements and those advanced by the Church today. A policy was here inaugurated which today has been readopted substantially unchanged.

Later legislative proposals, it will be noted, elicited considerable response and support from the ranks of organized labor. While concern for educational matters has already been attributed to the National Labor Union, its more powerful successor, the Knights of Labor (founded 1869) had not by 1870-1871 developed or enunciated an educational policy. Curoe notes only one other labor organization as expressing itself on educational legislation this early. This was the Colored National Labor Union, the first Negro labor organization, which at its convention in 1871 demanded that Congress enact a "national education law." Such a law, the union felt, was essential for the welfare and protection of the interests of labor.[26]

A description of the pressures for federal aid in general is not complete without consideration of the petitions received by Congress relative to the matter. The appearance of such petitions in discernible quantity coincides rather clearly with the cessation of the activities of the Freedmen's Bureau, and, since all such petitions originated in the South, one is tempted to surmise that they represented a measure of approval for the work of that agency. The third session of the Forty-first Congress (1870-1871) received thirty-two individual petitions on the subject of federal aid to education. Although ridiculously small in relation to the volume of contemporary pressures upon Congress, these petitions represent the beginning of a subsequently robust phenomenon. During this session, in which the Hoar bill was under consideration, twenty-seven of these petitions were rather general, ill-defined requests for aid, while the remaining five were concerned specifically with the Hoar bill. The great majority of these petitions was sent by groups of citizens in North Carolina and Tennessee, and none came from states out-

[26]Curoe, *op. cit.*, 75.

side the South. The typical petition asked Congress to secure for the children of the state "the inestimable blessings of a common school education," to "aid the common schools at the South," or for aid in the "establishment of common schools in the southern States." As noted earlier, it would be difficult to read into such requests a desire for a nationally administered and superimposed school system, but that some at least of the petitions meant just that can hardly be doubted.

Finally, it must be noted that the political parties had not yet committed themselves on the issue of federal participation in education. Neither platforms nor convention resolutions had yet deigned to consider education as a subject worthy of concern, and few leading politicians had indicated any interest in the subject. On the occasion of the formal ratification of the Fifteenth Amendment, however, President Grant found it necessary to take note of the educational implications of current conditions. His message to Congress on March 30, 1870, after alluding to the millions of newly freed and enfranchised Negroes, enjoined the legislators in these terms: "I would therefore call upon Congress to take all the means within their constitutional powers to promote and encourage popular education throughout the country."[27] Here, in effect, was the keynote for much of the educational policy of the Republican party for two decades.

PUBLIC PRESSURE FOR A NATIONAL SYSTEM OF EDUCATION

There were those whose belief in the essentiality of universal education led them to demand of Congress more specific enactments than have heretofore been mentioned. Curti notes that many educators believed, with the more extreme political reconstructionists, that education for the masses was a necessary safeguard to prevent Southern aristocracy from regaining its ascendancy. He quotes, for example, the president of Illinois Normal University as saying that the teacher "must finish what

[27]*Congressional Globe*, 49:1, 1735.

the soldier had so well begun."[28] Other state and local educational leaders shared this sentiment and the newly organized National Education Association* early went on record in favor of national aid and encouragement for Southern education. In the same vein, the *American Educational Monthly*, which was leading in the advocacy of the establishment of a federal education agency, continued its campaign for "national education." An editorial in April, 1867 staunchly championed a policy which would result in more nation-wide uniformity and standardization of educational activity. Such equalization, the magazine hoped, would result in the general improvement of American political life. Its concern with the curriculum of such a centrally controlled school system was, however, limited to the feeling that "A uniform system of this kind would challenge a degree of observation and criticism which few useless or antiquated studies could survive."[29] Among the first educational leaders to place himself on record as favoring a national system of education was the Superintendent of Schools for Michigan. He held that the Federal Government, in order to preserve democratic institutions and processes, had an imperative responsibility in the field of public education. His support, however, was tempered by the observation that a national system should be instituted to cooperate, not compete, with the state and local agencies, in order to "render them more widespread and effective."[30]

There were five petitions addressed to Congress relative to the bill or to its inherent principle—two from North Carolina, one each from Tennessee, Alabama, and Louisiana. All requested Congressional establishment of a system of public schools, and the last mentioned, that of Louisiana, represented the sentiments of an unrecorded number of members of the state legislature. Again, there is no assurance that request for such "estab-

[28]Merle Curti, *The Social Ideas of American Educators*, 210.
*Incorporated in 1869 as the National Educational Association. The name was changed in 1906 to the National Education Association of the United States. For clarity, the current title has been used throughout.
[29]"National Education," *American Educational Monthly*, 4:147, April, 1867.
[30]O. Horsford, in the *Report of the Commissioner of Education Made to the Secretary of the Interior for the Year 1870*, 413.

lishment" implied a desire for a federally controlled school system. It is equally conceivable that what was really being solicited was federal assistance in, but not supervision of, the institution and maintenance of public schools.

THE HOAR BILL: ITS PROVISIONS

On February 25, 1870, H.R. 1326, a bill "to establish a national system of education," was presented to the House of Representatives by George F. Hoar, Republican, of Massachusetts. This marked the opening of a struggle over the character of federal relations to education which was to continue with ever-increasing intensity for twenty years, a struggle destined to be the precursor of the debate in this area which has assumed even larger proportions in our own time. The Hoar bill, dealing specifically with common schools, was the first measure of its kind to receive Congressional consideration, if indeed it was not the first in this area to be proposed in an American Congress. It is noteworthy, too, that this bill, though the first, was in many respects more drastic than any which have followed; certainly the extremes which were here proposed have never been seriously considered in any subsequent legislative action.

What, then, did the Hoar bill propose? "The purpose of this bill, by which it is for the first time sought to compel by national authority the establishment of a thorough and efficient system of public instruction throughout the whole country, is not to supersede, but to stimulate, compel, and supplement action by the State."[31] So spoke Representative Hoar as he reported the bill from committee in June, 1870. The bill provided for the maintenance by national authority of a system of common school education. It was an attempt to make available for all children of school age the opportunity to receive instruction in basic arithmetic, reading, and writing, under federal auspices wherever a state failed to make such provision. The President was granted the authority to determine whether, in any state, a satisfactory school system was "in operation or in prospect."

[31]*Congressional Globe,* 41:2, 478.

Whenever he found a state thus delinquent, the bill asserted the right of the Federal Government to supply the deficiency.

Upon designation of a delinquent state, the President was given further authority to appoint a federal superintendent of schools for that state, while the Secretary of the Interior was responsible for appointing federal school inspectors for each Congressional district and for each local school district. National authority was provided for the building of schools and the appropriation of necessary property through eminent domain proceedings. Also, power to supervise the production of textbooks was lodged with the Federal Government. This establishment was to be supported by the levy of a direct annual tax, amounting to fifty cents per inhabitant, upon the delinquent states, which money would then constitute a federal fund from which distribution would be made according to the census data on illiteracy. In addition, the proceeds of the sales of certain public lands were to be devoted to the maintenance of a permanent school fund whose interest was to be similarly distributed.

In concluding his preliminary exposition of the bill, Hoar asked, "What, then, is the function of the national legislature?" He answered: "It is twofold. It is to compel to be done what the States will not do, and to do for them what they cannot do. . . . It must require a good and universal system of common-school education in those States which do not provide it. . . . The bill will only operate where the dominant power in any State refuses to provide education by local authority."[32] Later, in the course of the brief debate on the bill, Hoar was to remark: "I do not believe, if we should pass this law, that it will ever be necessary to put it in force. . . . I believe there is no State . . . but would at once establish a school system for itself."[33]

PUBLIC RESPONSE TO THE HOAR PROPOSAL

The reaction of the country to the suggestion of a national system of common schools, though of small proportions, was

[32]*Congressional Globe*, 41:2, 485.   [33]*Ibid.*, 41:3, 1042.

almost universally unfavorable. Even those who had been most energetic in proclaiming their advocacy of some form of federal assistance to educationally backward sections balked at the extremities to which the Hoar bill was committed. Even the few favorable comments upon the proposal, other than those made by its Congressional supporters, represented primarily mild endorsements of the purposes the bill was to accomplish rather than unequivocal approval of its methods. For example, one lay writer, reviewing the report of the educational exhibits at the recent Paris Universal Exposition and noting the "deficiencies" in amount and quality of American education in comparison with the education of north European countries, had this to say: "We hope [the Report] will be spread broadcast over our land, and carefully studied, especially at this moment, when Mr. Prosser's speech in the last Congress has brought to view the appalling state of things in many sections of the United States with respect to the deficiency of educational opportunities, and Mr. Hoar's bill for a national compulsory education to supplement the shortcomings of the State provisions is coming up for debate."[34]

Perhaps the strongest statement of approval for the bill, outside the halls of Congress, came, not unexpectedly, from the chairman of the Republican party's national committee. In an article in the *Atlantic Monthly*, whose continued interest in educational affairs throughout this period is noteworthy, this party spokesman placed education as "second to no question now before the country." The problems presented by reconstruction, enfranchisement of the Negro, immigration, and increasing illiteracy, he stated, allowed of no other conclusion. It was his conviction, therefore, that "the educational policy of the States which have hitherto sustained free schools should be substantially adopted by the nation," and that the Federal Government should have the power to enforce upon states the responsibility for the maintenance of free public schools. It was the duty of the American people and the Republican party to strengthen

[34]"Reviews and Literary Notices," *Atlantic Monthly*, 26:640, November, 1870.

the Bureau of Education and support a national system of education, as proposed in the Hoar bill, or "something tantamount thereto."[35]

The only organizational statement definitely approving the principles of the Hoar bill to come to the official attention of Congress was presented by the National Labor Union. Stepping beyond the generalized pronouncement of 1868, its convention of 1870 memorialized Congress "respectfully but earnestly . . . [for] early action in devising and enacting a national system of public school education, somewhat after the plan proposed" in the Hoar bill.[36] It was noted, at the time of the presentation of this memorial, that the membership of the National Labor Union was predominantly Southern.

Such rather limited commitments to the national system principle were heavily outweighed by the violent blasts of denunciation from the opponents of the scheme. Most forceful and vehement in opposition to the bill were several of the professional educational associations, led by the National Education Association. This organization, which only four years after its founding had become the spearhead for the design of much of the nation's educational policy, immediately took the lead in renouncing any allegiance to the new proposal. Professional antipathy toward the Hoar bill was admirably expressed in the address of J. P. Wickersham, the Superintendent of Common Schools for Pennsylvania, before the 1871 convention of the Association. His analysis of the bill found it "ill-advised and mischievous," "impractical and unAmerican." It was his contention that: (1) "The establishment of such a system is in opposition to the uniform practice of our National Government." (2) "It is in opposition to the wishes of the founders of the Republic and the leading statesmen of the nation." (3) "It is of doubtful constitutionality." (4) "It is in opposition to a sound republican political philosophy." Recognizing the extreme needs of the South for some sort of assistance in building up and sta-

[35]Henry Wilson, "New Departure of the Republican Party," *Atlantic Monthly*, 27:104-120, January, 1871.
[36]*Congressional Globe*, 41:3, 661.

bilizing its educational systems, however, Wickersham concluded his address by voicing his complete approval "of the
policy of the National Government's aiding public education
in the South by conditional appropriations of land and money."[37] Immediately following this statement, the convention
unanimously adopted this resolution: "Resolved: That this
Association will look with favor upon any plan giving pecuniary
aid to the struggling educational systems of the South, and that
the General Government may deem judicious."[38] In no sense
could this be construed as an endorsement of the Hoar bill, but
at the same time the Association's traditional advocacy of aid
to the South remained unimpaired.

This policy of complete non-support for the Hoar bill, coupled
with equally strong approval of less extreme measures of federal assistance, was typical of most educational groups and was
publicized both by association organs and by private professional magazines. The *National Teacher*, of which the former
Commissioner of Common Schools for Ohio, E. E. White, was
editor, deemed the Hoar proposals "inappropriate" and "unfor-
tunate." "We would rather suggest the policy of aiding and
stimulating the States to establish and maintain effective school
systems . . . [using] assistance, instead of compulsion."[39] It is at
this point and with the expression of identical sentiments that
a Southern professional journal appears on the scene, for the
organ of the Virginia teachers' association, though committed
to approval of federal aid, also found it necessary to condemn
the Hoar bill.[40]

The *Catholic World*, "in many respects the foremost of
American Catholic periodicals,"[41] felt constrained to place the
position of the Church on this issue squarely on the record. In
April, 1871, ostensibly in rebuttal to the statement of the Repub-

[37]*Addresses and Journal of Proceedings of the National Educational Association Sessions of the Year 1871*, 21-23; *Report of the Commissioner of Education*,
1871, 412.

[38]*National Educational Association*, op cit., 1871, 49.

[39]*National Teacher*, 1:185, February, 1871.

[40]"The National Bureau of Education," *Educational Journal of Virginia*,
2:109, January, 1871.

[41]Frank Luther Mott, *A History of American Magazines*, III, 68.

lican party's national chairman, this journal detailed the dangers it saw in the national system idea. It found in this plan evidence of Republican desire to enforce unification and centralization of all public life, basically designed "to suppress Catholic education, gradually extinguish Catholicity in the country, and to form one homogeneous American people after the New England Evangelical type." The writers felt that education was purely a state concern, that therefore any nationalization would be unconstitutional, but admitted that state control of education meant that Catholics "will soon be strong enough to force the state legislatures to give them their proportion of the public schools supported at public expense. . . . We hold state authority is the only constitutional authority under our system to establish schools and provide for them at the public expense; but we could manage to get along with national denominational schools as well as others could. We could educate in our share of the public schools our own children in our own way, and that is all we ask."[42] Realistically, therefore, while strongly opposed to the national control of schools, the Church admitted its willingness to accept a program of federal aid provided such aid was shared by its parochial schools. Thus, on somewhat different bases, the Catholic Church and the public educators were together in opposition to the Hoar bill.

In general, the press had not yet become aware, or at least was not prepared to concede, that the issue of federal relations to education was worthy of its notice. Most newspapers in 1870-1871 carried no mention of either the educational problem or the effort of Congress to alleviate it. Some of the more prominent dailies, which featured purely reportorial accounts of Congressional activity, managed to note that the Hoar bill was under consideration. Such comment as did appear was concentrated almost exclusively in the Eastern and Southern urban dailies—little mention appeared in the Midwestern or Far-western press. Even in New York City, where characteristically the issue of education received more press coverage than elsewhere, the *Tribune* and the *Herald* were the only leading newspapers to

[42]"Unification and Education," *Catholic World*, 13:1-14, April, 1871.

pay even cursory attention to the Hoar bill. Throughout the year in which the proposal was under consideration, the *Times* and the *Evening Post* showed no interest whatever in the matter. Such notice as the *Herald* conceded was rather caustic: Under the heading "Congress Yesterday—Buncombe Day in the House," it noted "The project for a grand scheme of national education was discussed."[43] And later: "The House held a night session for debate on the bill to establish a national system of education. It was dull and dreary entertainment."[44] The New York *Tribune*, however, consistently concerned about and sympathetic to the implementation of the Negro's newly won rights, took occasion to note that the chief value of this debate was to publicize the "deplorable state of ignorance prevailing at the South" and to create a public awareness that the condition might demand some sort of federal action. The *Tribune* questioned the advisability of centralizing education "when all foreign educators . . . [praise] the fact that it is established and maintained voluntarily by the States and municipalities, without the interference or control of the General Government."[45]

Other newspapers were more outspoken in their opposition. The Providence, Rhode Island, *Journal* noted that some saw in the Hoar bill evidence of a calculated political plot. Quoting from what it called a "Democratic organ at Washington," the *Journal* noted that "Mr. Hoar's bill is one of the most insidious and dangerous of all plans for perpetuating radical rule yet conceived by the inventive genius of New England, and is therefore the one that ought to be most firmly resisted."[46] But bitterest of all were the criticisms leveled at the bill by certain Southern newspapers, of which the following is a good example: "The Radicals in both Houses yesterday, by different roads, were working to the accomplishment of a design which is to place in the hands of the Radical party the expenditure of an immense amount of money, almost unlimited patronage . . . [which will

[43]New York *Herald*, January 29, 1871, 6.
[44]*Ibid.*, February 18, 1871, 4.
[45]New York *Tribune*, February 10, 1871.
[46]Providence *Journal*, February 1, 1871, 3.

lead to] corruption and fraud. . . . I have reference to the bill to establish a system of national education, by which the country, and the South especially, is to be flooded with Yankee school books, which for the most part breathe lies, slanders, and moral poison, and Yankee teachers who will be nothing more than emisaries [sic] of the Radical party. This monstrous violation of the rights of the people and the States was boldly and ably opposed. . . . Its passage is not at all certain."[47]

Cubberley records that the bill "awakened much interest throughout the North, and was strongly endorsed,"[48] and Hoar, writing in 1872, noted that the bill "was extensively discussed in the newspapers."[49] It seems clear that, while some concern over the bill was elicited—more than had appeared in connection with any previous educational legislation—most of it was of an unsympathetic character. Influential endorsement of the bill or its principles outside of Congress was almost totally lacking, though subscription to the idea that Southern education needed assistance was constantly gaining adherents.

CONGRESSIONAL ACTION ON THE HOAR BILL[50]

At the time of the debate on the national education bill, the Republican party was in complete control of the national government. Grant, whose sympathies for the cause of Southern educational improvement have already been noted, was midway through his first term in the Presidency. Republican control of the Congress was enforced by the presence of many Republican representatives from Southern states which had not yet been

[47]Petersburg, Virginia, *Index*, February 11, 1871, 1. The term "Radicals" as used here referred to the extremist wing of the Republican party which advocated the severest of reconstruction measures in dealing with the South. This group was led by such men as Benjamin F. Butler of Massachusetts and Horace Greeley of the New York *Tribune*. See Arthur M. Schlesinger, *Political and Social Growth of the United States- 1852-1933*, 90 ff., 111 ff.

[48]Ellwood P. Cubberley, *Public Education in the United States: A Study and Interpretation of American Educational History*, 442.

[49]George F. Hoar, "Education in Congress," *Old and New*, 5:601, May, 1872.

[50]For the entire debate on the Hoar bill, see the *Congressional Globe*, 41:2, 478-486, and 41:3, 1376-7, 1371-3, Appendix: 77-80, 95-99.

returned to complete independence. Thus, in the House, the only body to consider the Hoar bill, the alignment stood at 170 Republicans and 73 Democrats. The course of the brief debate (it occupied parts of seven days) demonstrated, however, that on this issue the party in power had not achieved the solidarity that was characteristic of much of its reconstruction legislation and that was to feature some of its later endeavors in the educational domain.

The case for the establishment of a national system of education was most ably presented by Representative Hoar as he reported the bill out of committee on June 6, 1870 and as he defended it in the formal debate of January and February, 1871. The basic purpose of the bill as Hoar conceived it was to attempt to compel the states to establish satisfactory common schools and, where the states failed to do so, to authorize the Federal Government to provide them. He pointed to the returns of the preceding year's census which indicated that in the South "only one-fourth of the persons who are growing up to assume the functions of citizens will be able to read and write." He maintained that the very system of government under which the United States operated demanded that, as it guaranteed to every man "his equal share in the Government," there be some assurance that every man possessed "the capacity for the exercise of that share in the Government." Hoar saw in this legislation the most effective kind of "protection" for American economic interests: "No American statesman will be unwilling to give to the American workman the advantage in the great industrial competition which results from superiority of knowledge." In the course of the debate, he was forced to cite constitutional authority for the proposal. He found that authority in two places: in Article I, Section 8—the "general welfare" and "necessary and proper" clauses—and in Article IV, Section 4, which guarantees to each state a "Republican form of Government." Hoar declared that the only criterion to be applied in adjudging a bill's constitutionality lay in the answer to the question: "Is the exercise of this power by the nation essential, indispensable to the maintenance of republican government?"

Hoar was joined by Representative Washington Townsend, Republican, of Pennsylvania, in attributing to the solid Democratic opposition ulterior political motives. Hoar claimed that in many places (presumably in the South) "men are banding themselves together to resist the extension of education to the people . . . to crush all attempts to give them knowledge." Townsend was more specific. The Democratic party, he stated, "has already sounded its bugle-blast against popular education; it has voted against supplies to the Bureau of Education, and one of its leaders has given formal notice that when his party gets into power it will abolish the bureau. . . . That party knows that the greater the ignorance of the masses the greater its political power, and hence it denounces the light of education. . . ."

Those representatives who stood with Hoar agreed that it would be improper for the Federal Government to interfere in the educational activities of a state when those functions were satisfactorily performed. In the eyes of its proponents, a national system would operate only in those areas where minimum standards were not maintained, for whatever reasons, by the states themselves. In Hoar's words: "Nobody proposes not to permit the States of this Union to educate their people. But what is proposed is not to permit them not to do it."

Three Northern Democrats led the opposition to the Hoar bill—John Bird of New Jersey, Thompson McNeely of Illinois, and Michael Kerr of Indiana. Their objections, and those of their followers, can be summarized as follows:

1. The proposal was totally unconstitutional. While approving a policy of aid by land or money grants, they could find no authority in the Constitution for establishing systems of schools. "The power to encourage education within the States is very different from the power to regulate and control it," proclaimed McNeely, and he noted further that, if this sort of operation was constitutional under the general welfare clause, "there is no limitation upon the power of the Federal Government whatever."

2. Such a program would offer unlimited opportunities for fraud, corruption, and political patronage. The President's pow-

er over state educational functions, federal authority in the matters of textbook publication and school building construction, and the large number of federal employees to be appointed would all conspire to defeat the purpose for which the bill was framed.

3. A national system must be based, as in their eyes the Hoar scheme was, upon a considerable degree of centralization of operation and standardization of procedure. The opposition found these to be undesirable, even un-American elements. This bill, said Bird, "takes the system of education entirely away from the people. To be efficient, the work of education must be domestic, free, self-imposed; not foreign, forced, compulsory." According to Kerr, the bill empowered Congress to require states to maintain educational systems "of the same kind, order, and completeness."

4. There had been no public demand for such legislation.

5. To expect Southern institutions to have regained their prewar effectiveness or to compare favorably with those of the North so soon after the Civil War was ridiculous and unrealistic. McNeely took occasion to note that under the Hoar bill, if it became law, the schools of New England would doubtless be found deficient, in view of the prevalence there of excessive child labor. He opined that "The uneducated plowboy of Tennessee, with no teacher but nature, has reason to thank his God that he is not an over-worked Massachusetts factory child."

6. The national system idea is basically one phase of a Republican plot to cement that party's political control. The opposition, notably Midwestern and Southern, here evidenced a traditional hatred and suspicion of the long-lived political domination of New England. "This proposition," said Kerr, "is a New England idea and policy . . . [characterized by] peculiar statesmanship . . . cunning selfishness . . . and cruel sectionalism." Bird feared that the teachers under the proposed system would become "political missionaries. Will not fifty-thousand New England school-teachers scattered throughout the South be able to control the vote?"

No votes of any kind were taken during this debate, but a

certain alignment is nevertheless discernible. The proponents of the bill were apparently exclusively Republican. The opposition, however, while led by the Democrats, could show a sizable number of Republican adherents. It is significant, too, that many of the Republican supporters of the bill were from Southern states whose status was still that of a defeated enemy country. Hoar, in reviewing this debate one year later, admitted that it was "quite doubtful whether it would have got through the House," and noted that it was allowed to "disappear" at the close of the session.[51] It seems clear that, in the absence of reconstruction-regimes in the South, the ultimate defeat of such a bill would have been even more certain.

Despite Representative Hoar's vigorous championship of the national education bill, there remains some question as to his basic motivation and that of his supporters on this measure. He professed considerable concern for educational affairs—the fight over the Bureau of Education, he wrote in his autobiography, "led me to give special study to the matter of national education," and yet, in that autobiography of over nine hundred pages, only one page is devoted to his efforts to enlist federal support for education. Elsewhere in his memoirs he describes his assignment to various Congressional committees, including the Committee on Education and Labor, as "obscure and unimportant"; only the Judiciary Committee "had any attraction for me."[52] He steadfastly maintained, after the national education bill had been allowed to die, that his only purpose in proposing it was to publicize the issue of educational need throughout the nation. It "was not drawn or introduced," he wrote, "with any confident expectation that it would get through Congress," but rather to stimulate interest in the problem and indicate the practicability and constitutionality of a law authorizing nationally administered schools if states failed to provide adequate educational facilities.[53] One is tempted to conclude that in every respect his purpose was left unachieved. The fact that

---

[51]Hoar, in *Old and New*, 5:601, May, 1872.
[52]Hoar, *Autobiography of Seventy Years*, 265 ff.
[53]Hoar, in *Old and New*, 5:600, May, 1872.

never again has a measure similar to this one been proposed seems to demonstrate that doubts as to the constitutionality of such a procedure have continued to exist. With regard to the stimulation of concern for the problem, somewhat more can be said, for in the next session of Congress a milder proposal for aid to education was passed by the House. It was not until ten years had elapsed, however, that public interest could be said to have been stimulated sufficiently to force serious Congressional consideration of the problem. It is not unlikely that, had there been advanced in 1870-1871 a more moderate, less controversial program, much of subsequent educational development would have been markedly different.

THE HOAR BILL: SUMMARY

Analysis of the proposal to establish a national system of education, in relation to its own time and to the subsequent history of federal relations to education, indicates that the following points are significant:

1. The Hoar bill was the first proposal that the Federal Government participate in common school education to receive serious Congressional consideration. While not, basically, a measure of federal aid or assistance, its introduction precipitated concern for the educational problem and for the function of the national government in relation thereto.

2. Although the Hoar bill was not the result of public pressure and did not elicit any considerable public response, it did produce the beginnings of professional interest and involvement in the issue of the relation of the Federal Government to education. It also brought about the enunciation of the policy of the Catholic Church with regard to this issue.

3. Consideration of the Hoar bill forced the profession to develop more definite conceptions as to the form and function of a federal policy for education. Among educators and laymen, a decided antipathy toward national control of education appeared.

4. The Hoar bill was an extreme proposal to deal with an ex-

treme situation. Its very extremity precluded any thoroughly intelligent discussion of the basic educational problem. The major concerns of the bill's critics were not with the educational aspects of the measure, but rather with its constitutionality and its actual or potential infringement of states' rights, its political undesirability, and with the belief that this was unprincipled sectional rather than genuinely national legislation.

5. While Congressional activity with regard to the Hoar bill reflected the general indifference in Congress toward educational affairs, the debate gave evidence of developing partisan positions on the issue of federal participation in education. Such partisan differences as are apparent, however, arose primarily over issues of constitutionality and concentration of power, and not over consideration of educational policy.

6. The Hoar bill represents the only significant attempt to legislate a nationally controlled and administered system of local schools.

7. The Hoar bill can justly be considered the beginning of the ensuing twenty-year battle for federal aid to common school education. Continued references to this bill in subsequent debates indicate that its influence upon educational thought was considerable. It is apparent, however, that the radical principle embodied in the Hoar bill was so directly contrary to the educational mores that a totally different approach was essential, if the problem were to be met. The next chapter turns, therefore, to a consideration of the first of the two major alternatives proposed by interested legislators as the basic pattern for federal participation in common school education.

· IV ·

THE ATTEMPTS TO AID COMMON SCHOOLS BY THE DIRECT APPLICATION OF THE REVENUES FROM PUBLIC LAND SALES: 1872-1880

THE PROPOSALS ADVANCED IN CONGRESS

Overview of the Period 1872-1880

BETWEEN the "disappearance" of the bill to establish a national common school system in February, 1871 and the first of the several attempts to authorize direct appropriations of money from the federal treasury to aid common schools in June, 1882, there appeared an intermediate stage of legislative activity. This can be characterized as an effort to supplement local common school funds through the application of the proceeds of public land sales to common school education. The extreme policies underlying the Hoar bill had apparently been discredited and discarded, but the need for educational improvement continued to grow more intense. Beginning with the next Congress, therefore, a new departure was inaugurated, one which seemed to give promise of answering the objections manifested in the Hoar bill debate and which had a degree of precedent in its support.

The eight-year period (roughly the 1870's) under consideration in this chapter was not marked by a constant or continued growth of concern for and familiarity with the problem of education on the part of Congress. Indeed, not until 1884-1885, in the 48th session of the Congress, did the number of federal aid bills introduced exceed that of the 41st Congress to which the Hoar bill had been presented. On the contrary, to judge by the record of bills introduced, Congressional interest in this area waned during the 1870's to the point where only one bill dealing with federal assistance to common schools was presented to each of the six Congresses in session from 1873 to 1880. Of a total of eleven bills introduced to Congress (between 1872 and 1880) designed to provide some form of federal assistance to local common schools, only four reached the floor and only two were considered, one by each House. Each of these two, however, was passed by the House in which it originated but failed of consideration in the other chamber. It is with these two bills, and with the environment of opinion which surrounded them, that this chapter is concerned.

The Perce Bill: Its Provisions[1]

On January 15, 1872, Legrand W. Perce, Republican, of Mississippi, introduced in the House of Representatives a bill "to establish an educational fund, and to apply the proceeds of the public lands to the education of the people." The opening section of the bill succinctly announced the principle upon which this and later similar bills were based: "the net proceeds of the public lands are hereby forever consecrated and set apart for the education of the people." Subsequent sections of the Perce bill provided that annually the proceeds of public land sales were to be halved, that one half was to be invested in government bonds yielding 5 percent interest, which investment was to constitute "a perpetual fund in the Treasury of the United States, to be known as the national education fund." The interest on this investment plus the other half of the revenue from land sales was to be distributed annually to the states, territories, and the District of Columbia upon the basis of their respective populations. States and territories were declared eligible to receive their shares of these moneys if, by a prescribed date, each had "engaged that it will provide by law for the free education of all its children between the ages of six and sixteen years, and will apply all moneys which it shall receive under this act in accordance with its conditions." The additional conditions required that all moneys thus obtained should "be solely applied to teachers' wages," that with-

[1] *Congressional Globe*, 42:2, 535-536, 795, 858.

in the states and territories the money should be apportioned only to school districts maintaining free schools for at least three months during a year, and that the states and territories should report in full to Congress regarding the use to which these moneys were put and the amounts locally appropriated for educational activities. The bill further provided that, for the first year 50 percent and subsequently 10 percent of all such moneys might be devoted to the maintenance of institutions for the training of common school teachers. Finally, the Commissioner of Education was granted the authority to certify the eligibility of the receiving units, his decisions being subject to appeals to Congress.

Amendments which were approved by the House revised the bill in three important particulars. The bill's original designation of *total* population as the basis for distribution of the money was amended to provide that distribution be based upon the population between the ages of four and twenty-one years. A further change, however, provided that for the first ten years the basis for distribution to the states and territories be that of their relative illiteracy, as indicated by the last census. A third significant amendment provided that no funds were to be withheld from a state or territory on the grounds that its laws provided separate schools for different races or prohibited "mixed" schools. Thus, "free" schools as written in the law was not to be construed as requiring that all schools be open to all children. This last proviso was of considerable importance since with it, in effect, official recognition of the Southern requirement of a dual school system was accomplished. No subsequent consideration of legislation designed to aid common schools has been able to ignore this issue, and contemporary educators and legislators must continue to face it.

The Burnside Bill: Its Provisions[2]

On March 29, 1879, Senator Ambrose E. Burnside, Republican, of Rhode Island, presented to the Senate a bill "to establish an educational fund and apply a portion of the proceeds of the public lands to public education and to provide for the more

[2]*Congressional Record*, 46:1, 147.

complete endowment and support of national colleges for the advancement of scientific and industrial education." This bill had substantial similarities with the earlier Perce bill, but differed in one fundamental aspect. While it devoted the proceeds of public land sales, together with the surplus revenues of the Patent Office, to education, the Burnside bill provided that *all* such moneys be invested in United States bonds to constitute a permanent educational fund. Thus only the interest on the investment was to be available for annual distribution. Like the Perce bill as finally passed, the distribution of this money to the states and territories was to be based on the illiteracy rates of persons over ten years of age for the first ten years of the operation of the law. Subsequently all distribution was to be made according to the relative populations between the ages of five and twenty-five. Another, though less significant, difference was a provision that one-third of the money annually available for distribution be granted to the land-grant colleges, this to continue until the income of each college equaled $30,000 per year, after which the entire interest obtained from the bonds would be devoted to common schools. Provisions empowering the Commissioner of Education with discretionary authority over distribution of the fund and requiring reports from the states and territories were almost identical with those in the Perce proposal. Amendments were approved which authorized the use of a portion of the grants for the training of common school teachers and authorized the land-grant colleges to establish "schools for the instruction of females in such branches of technical or industrial education as are suited to their sex."

These two proposals mark the chronological limits of this secondary stage in the over-all battle to legislate federal aid for common school education. It is worthy of note that, as evidenced by the bills themselves, the idea of a national system of education had been totally repudiated by educational legislators. Significant, too, is the return to the procedure instituted by the Morrill Act of 1862, by this time apparently accepted and recognized as legitimate by a considerable majority in Congress, that of using the income from public land sales in behalf of education. Only the procedure, however, was established; the acceptability of its application to common school education had yet to be tested.

PUBLIC PRESSURE WITH REGARD TO FEDERAL AID TO COMMON SCHOOL EDUCATION

It would be a mistake to conclude that Congressional inactivity with regard to aid to education during the 1870's was altogether a reflection of public apathy or unconcern. On the contrary, professional and public interest in this question persisted and tended to grow increasingly explicit. It was the Forty-fifth Congress, meeting from 1877 to 1879, when no federal aid measures were under consideration, that received by far the largest number of petitions on this subject of any Congress during the decade. While it is true that the profession and, to some extent, the Congress, were in the early 1870's concerned about the possibility of establishing a national university, and that in the middle and late 1870's profession, public, and Congress were occupied with the issue of sectarianism in education, nevertheless a steady undercurrent of interest in and demand for federal aid legislation was maintained. This continued expression of individual and, still to a very limited extent, of organized group concern in the 1870's contributed much to the development of a climate of opinion in the 1880's in which it would have been almost impossible to ignore the problem any longer.

The General Public

Public interest in a national program of educational assistance can perhaps be measured with some adequacy by a study of the petitions received by Congress during the 1870's. It was not until late in the decade, however, that these expressions reached any sizable volume. The Perce bill itself elicited almost no response of this character. During its brief consideration, a few memorials were received by both Houses, stimulated doubtless by the Hoar proposal, requesting the establishment of a "national system of public schools." Only two petitions were registered by Congress during this debate which requested "aid in establishing schools" and but one—from the German-American Teachers' Association—recommending the application of land sale proceeds to education.

As noted earlier, it was the Forty-fifth Congress, in session from late 1877 through the spring of 1879, when no federal aid legislation was under consideration, which received the most intensive aggregation of petitions and memorials on the subject of federal aid legislation. Indeed, no previous Congress had been so insistently pressured with regard to any form of educational legislation. The *Congressional Record* registers sixty petitions and memorials as having been presented to this Congress on this matter. Of these, all but six originated in Southern states, and none were received from any state west of Wisconsin. The Southern petitions (which represented all of the South except Virginia, West Virginia, Tennessee, Louisiana, Mississippi, and Texas) were almost exclusively devoted to requests for aid to be derived from the sales of public lands. Nearly one-half of these requests originated in Alabama and over one-fifth were sent from Missouri. The few Southern representations which did not specifically mention the public lands as the source for aid, but asked rather for the establishment of a fund or merely for assistance in establishing schools, may well have meant to imply the use of land sales for this purpose. It seems clear, at any rate, that whatever Southern opinions were reflected in this manner were overwhelmingly in favor of the policy proposed by the Perce bill and later by the Burnside bill.

No generalization on the basis of the six Northern-born petitions is warranted except mention of the obvious—the almost total absence of public interest in the federal aid problem. Only one of the six was of Eastern origin; the others were Middlewestern expressions. In general, these petitions indicate a concern that the Bureau of Education be strengthened, and suggest that proposals for moderate assistance to education on the part of the national government would have been favorably received.

The Forty-sixth Congress, during which the Senate considered the Burnside bill, received but scant attention from petitioners for federal assistance to education. While the petitions received by the previous Congress doubtless contributed somewhat to the favorable consideration of the bill by the Senate, it is impossible to account for the almost complete cessation of such appeals at a time when there was some prospect of attaining their objective. While it might be said of some sections of the country that public opinion was sufficiently aroused, certainly national concern over federal aid had hardly begun to be apparent. It is appropriate, therefore, to turn now to consider the expressions on this issue of certain of the major social groups, beginning with farmers' organizations.

The National Grange

In 1867, there had appeared among farmers an organization, known as the Patrons of Husbandry or the Grange, which, as a result of the depression of 1873, became an active economic and political agency for the advancement of agricultural interests. As the only major farm group operative in the 1870's, the degree and direction of its interest in education and federal aid are of some significance. In its "Declaration of Purposes" the Grange had committed itself to support of public education thus: "We shall advance the cause of education among ourselves, and for our children, by all just means within our power."[3] It would appear, however, that whatever concern for common school education was evidenced by the Grange was wholly unrelated to the issue of federal assistance. Periam[4] and Curoe[5] indicate that the organization expressed considerable interest in agriculture—what it considered "practical"—education and that this led it to endorse warmly the Morrill Act; here, notes Curoe, in its relation to the land-grant colleges, appeared "perhaps the most definite policy of the Grange" with respect to education. Apparently, the Grange conceived of the common school problem as lying entirely within a framework of state responsibility, and

[3]E. A. Allen, *Labor and Capital*, 435.
[4]Jonathan Periam, *The Groundswell: A History of the Origins, Aims, and Progress of the Farmers' Movement.*
[5]Philip R. V. Curoe, *Educational Attitudes and Policies of Organized Labor in the United States*, 95-96.

its efforts for common school improvement, which in the 1870's were not extensive, did not take any cognizance of the proposals to make federal funds available.

The Knights of Labor

A similar absence of awareness of or interest in the federal aid to education issue was characteristic of the major labor organization of the 1870's, the Knights of Labor. Laborers and farmers alike were undoubtedly too preoccupied with their own more immediate economic problems to be able to afford concern for such an issue. Like the Grange, the Knights of Labor held a deep faith in the value of the common schools, viewing them as essentially a medium of preparation for the skilled trades and an agency for training in the responsibilities of citizenship.[6] The organization's interest in federal aid, however, was limited to demands for nationally sponsored agencies which would counteract the "medieval economics" and the anti-union philosophies presented by the established colleges.[7]

The Knights of Labor was essentially weak in terms of developing or acting upon any general educational policies. There were long periods in its history when no concern of any kind was expressed for education at any level, and at no time did the organization institute committees to study the relation of the labor movement to educational developments. Curoe, having reviewed Terence V. Powderley's claims of the achievements of the Knights of Labor, found nothing in the nature of "specific educational accomplishments."[8] But, Curoe notes later in his extensive survey of organized labor's educational attitudes, ". . . a large expert interest in education on the part of organized labor is not to be expected. Down to the American Federation of Labor, or more properly, to the accession of the teachers to the Federation, such an interest is not to be found. But labor groups *have* helped to furnish some of the 'drive' behind educational changes at many points in our history."[9]

[6]Curoe, *op. cit.*, 80.
[7]*Ibid.*, 88-89.
[8]*Ibid.*, 91.
[9]*Ibid.*, 190.

The Educational Profession

Senator Hoar, in the course of the debate on the Burnside bill in 1880, claimed that the bill had received the "substantially unanimous accord" of the educators of the nation. While it was true that there was considerable professional support for the principle upon which the Burnside bill was based, the implication that the profession was solid and united in its favor was wholly unwarranted. Influential professional voices were heard on both sides of this issue.

The two most vehement champions of federal aid to common school education, and particularly aid through the use of land sale proceeds during the 1870's were the National Education Association and the Bureau of Education. It was noted in the previous chapter that, at its 1871 convention, the National Education Association in refusing support to the Hoar bill resolved in favor of "any plan of giving pecuniary aid to the struggling educational systems of the South, that the General Government may deem judicious." In November, 1871, the Commissioner of Education, John Eaton, offered one of the earliest, if not the first, official suggestion that federal aid to common schools be financial in form and based upon land sales. In his report for the year 1871, Eaton noted the continuing and increasing need in the South for assistance, and recommended the placement of public land sale proceeds in a special school fund whose principal or interest should be distributed where needed according to Congressional direction.[10] He elaborated his stand by stating: "No interference with local rights is suggested. But the offer of pecuniary aid to the amount of ten or fifteen thousand dollars for each congressional district, on condition that a certain amount shall be raised by local means, and free common schools be opened for the benefit of all, would constitute a motive which would stimulate the friends of education in those communities, so as to render well-nigh universal the sentiment in favor of such schools."[11] It is noteworthy, too, that this proposal

[10]*Report of the Commissioner of Education for the Year 1871*, 74.
[11]*Ibid.*, 9.

advanced the idea that has since gained considerable status, the principle of "matching" or "dollar for dollar" operation, in the belief that only thus would federal aid stimulate rather than reduce local efforts for education.

The National Education Association was quick to echo General Eaton's sentiments and to proclaim its advocacy of federal aid in more specific terms than had its previous pronouncements. The passage of the Perce bill by the House of Representatives offered an opportunity and the Association promptly responded. Its convention of 1872 unanimously adopted a resolution which proclaimed, in view of the Perce bill's non-interference with "the constitutional or traditional relations" between the federal government and the states, and its presumed stimulus to private and local efforts, that the Association "heartily commends" the House of Representatives and enthusiastically endorses the bill.[12] In its conventions of 1873, 1874, and 1875, the Association re-affirmed its commitment to the urgency of federal assistance to education and its approval of a policy of devoting the public lands to that end. While the convention of 1876 was presented with a similar resolution, there is no record of its having been brought to a vote. The Association from 1877 to 1880, however, published no resolutions dealing with federal aid, except occasional pronouncements favoring a national university.

Despite the general antagonism to federal aid which characterized the leadership of the private colleges, which will presently be noted, the advocates of national assistance received some unexpected support from James McCosh, the President of Princeton University. Addressing the National Education Association in 1873, McCosh flatly opposed the government support of higher education which had begun with the Morrill Act —this, in his view, was merely another opportunity for "political jobbing." He did, however, take occasion to voice his approval of the creation from land sale proceeds of a permanent school fund, the interest of which should be devoted to the support of high schools primarily. Recognizing the acute needs of the

[12]*The Addresses and Journal of Proceedings of the National Educational Association, 1872*, 108.

South, he agreed that in that region the common schools too should share in the fund.[13]

During the 1870's, the profession's most outspoken critic of the idea of federal aid to education, apparently regardless of the basis upon which it was proposed, was President Charles W. Eliot of Harvard University. Unsympathetic, as was McCosh, with the program of aid to higher education, and even more bitterly opposed to the establishment of a national university, Eliot found no good to be obtained from national aid to common school systems. Repeatedly, and with great vehemence, he voiced his complete antipathy to any and all such programs. "The fatal objection to this subsidizing process is that it saps the foundations of public liberty. The only adequate securities of public liberty are the national habits, traditions, and character acquired and accumulated in the practice of liberty and self-control," Eliot told the National Education Association at its 1873 convention.[14] He continued: "Let us cling fast to the genuine American method—the old Massachusetts method—in the matter of public instruction. The essential features of that system are local taxes for universal elementary education voted by the citizens themselves, local elective boards to spend the money raised by taxation and control the schools, and for the higher grades of instruction permanent endowments administered by incorporated bodies of trustees. This is the American voluntary system. . . . [which] breeds freemen."[15] Eliot maintained that perhaps universal elementary education provided by the State was justifiable as "a cheap system of police for the national defense," but he utterly rejected any program which would tax one man to send another's sons to high school or college.[16] While it is, of course, impossible to assess the extent of Eliot's influence, it is safe to assume that the prestige of his position lent great weight to his public utterances. It is certain that,

[13]John A. H. Keith and William C. Bagley, *The Nation and Its Schools*, 107-108.

[14]Keith and Bagley, *op. cit.*, 111.

[15]Charles W. Eliot, "A National University," *Popular Science Monthly*, 3:691-692, October, 1873; also *A National University*, 22.

[16]Frank W. Blackmar, *The History of Federal and State Aid to Higher Education*, 35.

among leaders of private colleges and universities, there existed considerable support for the views he expressed.

Public educators, too, however, were to be found within the ranks of the opposition. Despite the National Education Association's resolutions and official Bureau of Education policy statements, many public school leaders remained unconvinced. One of the more eminent of these was the Secretary of the Connecticut State Board of Education, B. G. Northrop. Writing in 1879, Northrop maintained that public opinion was continually "growing in favor of the unfettered working of the State [school] systems, that this has now become our settled policy, which no lobby in Washington can change if it would, and should not if it could." He then proceeded to ask: "In the light of such facts, and in view of the rapid working of intellectual forces in this age and country, and the growing power of public sentiment, shall the most illiterate portions of our land be reached by NATIONAL schools supported by National aid and in any way controlled by a National Department? Shall the National Bureau of Education become a Federal Department, enlarged and authorized to organize and maintain a National University—or with still greater expansion, empowered to establish schools and distribute the income from the sale of public lands. . . ?" And finally, "Should the admitted school destitution of the South . . . be promptly removed by any federal agency, or more gradually supplanted by developing a proper local public sentiment?"[17]

State educational organizations in many instances evidenced coolness if not active antipathy toward federal aid proposals. The programs, resolutions, and publications of many professional associations during the 1870's reveal no activity in support of such policies; on the basis of this evidence, some might be cited for indifference. It is significant that, amid the extremities of reconstruction, the Georgia Teachers' Association could resolve (in 1873): "That in view of the educational wants of Georgia it is, in the opinion of this Association, our duty to encourage

[17]B. G. Northrop, *Schools and Communism, National Schools, and Other Papers*, 14-17.

and strive to promote a system of free public schools in our State."[18] Neither this resolution nor the proceedings of the convention by which it was adopted give any indication that federal aid for Georgia's schools was considered by this group to be a possible or a desirable approach to the solution of the problem. That this was typical of much of Southern professional thinking is not an unwarranted inference, as many Southern responses to the legislative proposals of the 1880's were to demonstrate.

Perhaps the most conclusive evidence that the educational profession in the 1870's was uncertain about and in part hostile to the idea of federal aid appears in a statement prepared by Duane Doty, the Superintendent of Schools of Detroit. Doty was asked by the Commissioner of Education to summarize the American professional consensus on educational matters, which summary became a part of the United States Government exhibit at an international exposition held in Vienna. The statement was approved by over one hundred of the leading American educators, and, while it makes no mention of, hence no commitment relative to federal aid as a principle, the essential core of a reliance upon local initiative and local effort in the advancement of education is a cardinal feature. Doty wrote:

Upon the several States individually, in which is vested the power of defining the qualifications of the electors who choose by ballot the representatives that make and execute the laws of the land, rests the responsibility of making provision for the education of those charged with the primary political functions of life. . . . Military education for the Army and Navy only has been directly provided for by the national Government. . . . To the several States individually is left . . . the establishment of public agencies for the well being of the civil and social community in its industrial, economical, social, and spiritual aspects.[19]

The educational profession was not yet united in support of, nor clear in its conception of, the principle of federal assistance to education.

[18]*Proceedings of the Seventh Annual Meeting of the Georgia Teachers' Association*, 1873, 35.
[19]Duane Doty, *A Statement of the Theory of Education in the United States of America as approved by many leading educators*, 9.

The Catholic Church

While many religious denominations had participated actively in the private attempts to improve educational conditions in the South, little official interest in the consideration of national measures to meet those conditions was evidenced by most of the established churches. The campaign of the Catholic Church, however, stimulated by the introduction of the Hoar bill, was vigorously maintained. Throughout the decade statements appeared which served to highlight further the Catholic position.

Earlier Catholic statements had professed acceptance of, if not belief in, the common school system, and a reluctant willingness to participate in federal aid programs if they should be established. Subsequent to the demise of the Hoar bill, however, the policy of noncommittal support of public schools and federal assistance for them seems to have been abandoned. The Church's traditional faith in the right of the Church alone to regulate and provide education was reaffirmed. Complete denial was expressed to the proposition that "whatever affects the prosperity of the State ought of necessity to belong to the jurisdiction of the civil power." On the contrary, "Education is not within the jurisdiction of earthly governments. It is above their competence." Therefore, "The superintendence and direction of the public schools . . . belong of right to the Catholic Church." Recognition of this truth, it was maintained, would result in "peace and concord . . . and every one, content with his position here on earth, because his hopes are on high, is more intent on making himself better than on overthrowing existing institutions that he may raise himself on their ruins."[20]

Upon such a base, support of governmental aid for education was impossible. Thus Orestes Brownson wrote that the government "has no authority to legislate . . . on the subject of private rights, on religion or morality, on education. . . ."[21] The right of

---

[20]"Unification and Education," *Catholic World*, 13:5, April, 1871; "The Rights of the Church over Education," *Catholic World*, 21:732-737, September, 1875.

[21]Orestes A. Brownson, "Politics at Home," *Brownson's Quarterly Review*, 1:100, January, 1873.

the State to require that all children be educated, or to provide education when parents were delinquent was conceded, "but it can itself neither educate, nor determine what education may or may not be given in them [the schools]." Nor can the State "tax the whole people, or use funds belonging to the whole people, to establish and sustain schools which only part, though by far the larger part, of the people, can use with a good conscience."[22] One Catholic editorialist, after accusing the other religious denominations of promoting public schools as an anti-Catholic conspiracy, proposed two alternatives to the current common school system. The first was that Catholic and other denominational schools be supported by public funds in the proportion that their student number bore to the public school population. But the second alternative, which the writer considered more desirable, was the abolition of all school taxation, hence of the public schools themselves, returning the educational responsibility to the confines of the family.[23] While the legislative developments of the 1870's were not such as to force the Catholic Church to pronounce specifically upon concrete proposals for federal aid to education, the position of the Church with regard to the principle was not left in doubt. The stand taken by the Catholic leadership was one of complete disapproval of any federal support of public education.

The Political Parties

From the point of view of its usefulness as a national political issue, as well as that of its increased recognition as a governmental problem, education began to come into its own during the 1870's. Both the major parties, the Republican party more extensively but no more explicitly than the Democratic party, placed themselves squarely on the record with regard to federal aid. At least one minor party expressed itself on this issue, going far beyond the pronouncements hitherto made by the major political organizations.

[22]*Ibid.*, 290, 294.
[23]"Who Is to Educate Our Children?" *Catholic World*, 14:433-437, January, 1872.

THE REPUBLICAN PARTY

It was not in its platforms, however, that the Republican party's growing devotion to the principle of national aid was made evident. The platform of 1872 made no mention of education but was careful to reaffirm the party's concern for the maintenance of states' rights. First mention of education in any Republican party platform appeared in that of 1876, where, after proclaiming its faith in the public schools as the "bulwark of the American Republic," the party recommended an amendment to the Constitution prohibiting the use of public funds or property "for the benefit of any schools or institutions under sectarian control."[24]

Other election-year statements of the Republican party were more specific. One campaign document cited the "devotion" of the Republican party to education and maintained that "Amidst Democratic hatred, opposition and denunciation, the Republicans have persevered in their beneficent legislation for these purposes. It was they who . . . [here several items of federal aid to specific local educational efforts were listed], instituted a Department of Education, . . . [and] have set apart the proceeds of the public lands for the support of public schools."[25] This last claim, based on the passage of the Perce bill by the House of Representatives, was most premature, but it served to indicate continued Republican commitment to the federal aid idea. In a campaign pamphlet addressed primarily to labor, much was made of the Republican belief in and support of such aspects of education as female seminaries, vocational training, and higher pay for teachers, although no expression of definite national educational policy appeared.[26] But it is not the absence of such an explicit statement that is significant, rather the evidence of recognition by the party that the question of public education carried political appeal and, again, the subscription by the party to support of the public school movement.

[24]George D. Ellis, *Platforms of the Two Great Political Parties*, 45.
[25]*One Hundred Reasons Why Every Man Should Vote for the Reelection of President Grant*, 5.
[26]*The Republican Party the Workingman's Friend*, 1-8.

It is, however, in the official statements of the decade's two Republican Presidents, Grant and Hayes, that the clearest indications of party policy are to be found. While one hesitates to conclude that such Presidential statements represented either the official party policy or the sentiments of a party majority, there can be no doubt that these pronouncements, and especially those of Grant, carried great weight with the Republican rank and file. It should be noted, moreover, that the influence of such statements was not confined to the year or the Presidential term in which they were made; they were not forgotten in the great federal aid debates of the 1880's.

Few Presidents have been more explicit or more vigorous in their advocacy of federal concern for and support of public education than was U. S. Grant. His messages to Congress were replete with recommendations and requests for action in this area. In his Third Annual Message, delivered on December 4, 1871, he noted that "Educational interest may well be served by the grant of the proceeds of the sale of public lands to settlers. I do not wish to be understood as recommending in the least degree a curtailment of what is being done by the General Government for the encouragement of education."[27] Upon the passage by the House of the Perce bill in 1872, Grant commented in his Fourth Annual Message that it was a "measure of such great importance to our real progress and is so unanimously approved by the leading friends of education that I commend it to the favorable attention of Congress."[28] But it was in the message to Congress of December 8, 1875, that Grant presented his most complete and unequivocal commitment to the principle of federal concern for the public schools.

> . . . the education of the masses becomes of the first necessity for the preservation of our institutions. . . . As the primary step . . . I suggest . . . and most earnestly recommend it, that a constitutional amendment be submitted to the legislatures of the several States for ratification, making it the duty of each of the several States to establish and forever maintain free public schools adequate to the edu-

[27]James D. Richardson, *A Compilation of the Messages and Papers of the Presidents,* 1789-1897, VII, 152.
[28]*Ibid.,* 203.

cation of all the children in the rudimentary branches within their respective limits, irrespective of sex, color, birthplace, or religions; forbidding the teaching in said schools of religious, atheistic, or pagan tenets; [and guaranteeing that school funds would be spent only for schools].

At the close of this message, Grant recapitulated his recommendations by presenting a five-point program, of which the first question of "vital importance" for legislative concern was:

that the States shall be required to afford the opportunity of a good common-school education to every child. . . . no sectarian tenets shall ever be taught in any school supported in whole or in part by [public funds]. Make education compulsory, so far as to deprive all persons who cannot read and write from becoming voters after the year 1890. . . .[29]

It must be noted, however, that the extent to which Grant was willing to commit the Federal Government to support public education was not made clear. That the government should further and strengthen the public schools was his firm belief, and he never doubted that as education was improved political processes would be fortified. Toward the close of his second term, it became evident that his conception of federal aid to education did not embrace support of higher education. In an address to a gathering of Union Army veterans, he enjoined the country to "resolve that neither the state nor the nation, nor both combined, shall support institutions of learning other than those sufficient to afford every child . . . the opportunity of a good common-school education. . . ."[30]

President Hayes also expressed considerable concern for the matter of national support of education. Presiding during a period when Congressional interest in such legislation was at a low ebb, he nevertheless repeatedly called for Congressional recognition of the primacy of the educational question. In his first inaugural, Hayes noted that national prosperity depended upon the "intellectual and moral condition of the people." Therefore, he continued, "liberal and permanent provision should be made

[29]Richardson, *op. cit.*, 356.
[30]Quoted in John C. Henderson Jr., *Our National System of Education*, 116.

for the support of free schools by the State governments, and if need be, supplemented by legitimate aid from national authority."[31] Campaign literature prepared for the election of 1880 quoted Hayes as having urged Congress to "supplement the local educational funds in the several States where the grave duties and responsibilities of citizenship have been devolved on uneducated people" by devoting lands and moneys to education.[32] "No more fundamental responsibility rests upon Congress," he told that body in 1879, "than that of devising appropriate measures of financial aid to education, supplemental to local action in the states and territories. . . ."[33]

THE DEMOCRATIC PARTY

Until the Civil War, the Democratic party had subscribed to a policy regarding the public lands which was first enunciated in the platform of 1844: "Resolved. That the proceeds of the public lands ought to be sacredly applied to the national objects specified in the Constitution, and that we are opposed to . . . any law, for the distribution of such proceeds among the states, as alike inexpedient in policy and repugnant to the Constitution." Nothing in the post-war actions of the Democratic party had indicated any repudiation of this principle. It was not until 1876 that the Democratic party found it desirable to make specific mention of education in its platform. Simultaneously, in this platform, the party leadership reaffirmed its traditional avowal of the states' rights theory of governmental relationships and its rejection of the policy of federal aid to education. The Republican party was accused of raising "false issues" in the campaign, the first of which was described as "The false issue with which they would enkindle sectarian strife in respect to the public schools, of which the establishment and support belong exclusively to the several States, and which the Democratic party has cherished from their foundation, and is resolved to

[31]*Ibid.*, 75.

[32]Republican Congressional Committee, *The Republican Campaign Text Book for 1880*, 74.

[33]National Education Association, *Federal Support for Education: the Issues and the Facts*, Research Bulletin XV, No. 4, September, 1937, 159.

maintain . . . without largesses from the Treasury to any."[34]

Democratic party leaders, in general, shied away from commenting upon the federal aid issue. Recognizing that it was politically unwise to deny the existence of a public school problem, yet at the same time committed by the deepest conviction to the principle of state sovereignty and a strict reading of the Constitution, most Democrats must have found this question politically dangerous. Outside of Congress, then, there was little attempt on the part of the Democratic membership to argue the matter. In the election campaign of 1876, for example, it seems to have been left to the Vice-Presidential candidate, Thomas A. Hendricks, to deal with the issue of federal assistance to schools, and even his mention was cursory and indirect. "Of sectional contentions, and in respect to our common schools, I have only this to say: That in my judgment, the man or party that would involve our schools in political or sectarian controversy is an enemy to the schools. The common schools are safer under the protecting care of all the people than under the control of any party or sect."[35]

By the end of the 1870's, then, party policies were rather firmly established and, at least in the case of the Republican party, widely known. Traditional Democratic commitments and convictions forced that party to repudiate the concept that local education was a matter for national concern. Republican policy, on the contrary, whose roots were constantly nourished by the remembrance of a war to destroy those Democratic ideals, came more and more to consider federal aid to education as a necessary and vital element in the preservation of the governmental system. That education had begun to come of age politically seems evident. Repeatedly, Democrats were accused of opposing aid to education because of their fears of the effects of expanded educational opportunity upon their political status. Republicans, on the other hand, were charged with a desire to remove the responsibility for education from the people, as one

[34]Ellis, *op. cit.*, 41.
[35]Democratic Party National Committee, *The Campaign Text Book* (1876), 15-16.

phase of a scheme to effect ever more concentrated and centralized control of the entire national life. It is interesting to note
that neither party, in order to meet the challenge of this newly
discovered problem, found it necessary or expedient to modify
the traditional patterns contained in its statements of party
policy.

THE PROHIBITION PARTY

The one minor party which, according to Schlesinger, "managed to stay alive" during this period was the Prohibition party.
Its significance here does not lie in its influence upon contemporary affairs, which was negligible, but in the advanced position it occupied on the educational issue. Its platform of 1872,
appearing only three years after the party's founding, may well
have been the first platform of any party to evidence specific
concern for education. The platform's statement that "the fostering and extension of common schools is a primary duty of the
government" was probably the first political platform to declare,
in effect, in favor of federal aid to education.[36] This was followed, in 1876, by a platform which called for the "establishment, by mandatory provisions in national and state constitutions, and by all necessary legislation, of a system of free public schools, for the universal and forced education of all the
youth of the land," a declaration which was essentially advocacy
of the Hoar bill idea.[37] While the Prohibitionists were considerably in advance of the general public on the matter of compulsory public education, there is little doubt that many professional educators and laymen would have rejoiced to find a
statement of this tenor incorporated in the platform of a major
party.

The Press

In line with the increased public interest in the federal aid
question, the American press in the 1870's began to devote more

[36]Thomas Hudson McKee, *The National Conventions and Platforms of All
Political Parties: 1789 to 1900,* 158.
    [37]*Ibid.,* 176.

space to its consideration. Increasingly, magazines of some national weight recognized not only the importance but the newsworthiness of discussions of this issue. Newspapers, however, commented only sparingly and only while federal aid legislation was actually under consideration. As before, the interest of newspapers in this subject was confined to the journals of the Eastern seaboard; while some papers more distant from the Capital occasionally reported the introduction or passage of federal aid measures, most seemed to ignore it altogether.

Among magazines of this period, federal aid to education had its staunchest supporter in *Harper's Monthly*. Although its circulation by the early 1870's was in the neighborhood of 200,000, the magazine's influence upon public opinion has been placed in some doubt. Mott writes that *Harper's* "was anything but a 'journal of opinion,' except when an opinion was almost universally acceptable."[38] The viewpoints expressed by this magazine on the federal aid question may have been thought by the editors to be reflections of a clear majority sentiment. That they were not has already been demonstrated, but that they were indicative of a not inconsequential segment of public opinion seems undeniable.

Harper's writers believed in the essentiality of an elementary or common school education as basic to the proper functioning of American democracy. They were unable to find any valid difference in principle between federal support of colleges and aid to universal or general education. *Harper's* contributors could find no reason why the national government "should not provide for the common welfare by insisting upon the general education of the vast mass of our illiterates." They could find no defense for the proposition that the national government must not interfere in certain local areas, especially education. The question to be considered, they maintained, was not that of interference versus non-interference, but rather one of the "desirability" of the fruits of such federal activity. Feeling that the influx of illiterate immigrants and the continued illiteracy among

[38]Frank Luther Mott, *A History of American Magazines*, II, 392.

native Americans constituted a national danger, one writer protested that "The safety of the government requires that it should
enforce and support everywhere popular instruction. Where a
State fails to educate its people, the national government has
plainly a right to interfere, and a general system of public
instruction might be formed" to require universally "thorough
and practical teaching, uniformity in study, and mental equality
throughout the nation."[39]

The position of *Scribner's Monthly* during the 1870's was
neither so consistent nor so definite. This periodical, with a circulation of over 100,000 by 1880, is considered by Mott as having been particularly "strong, especially at the close of the
seventies, in the discussion of such themes as education. . . ."
Much of the writing on education was the work of the editor,
Josiah Gilbert Holland, whom Mott considers one "of the half-
dozen greatest American magazine editors."[40] Holland felt constrained to look askance at those proposals of national action in
education which involved compulsory school attendance. While
believing completely in public education, he questioned seriously the assumption that "the existing system is anywhere near
that state of perfection which would warrant us in stereotyping
it, and enforcing it on all children." Nevertheless, the editors of
Scribner's also maintained that one of the basic ills of the
country was the lack of a national educational policy. "There
are as many educational policies as there are States, each acting
entirely independent of all the others. ...We need a United States
law in regard to education applying alike to all States . . . [to]
provide an elementary education for every child in the land, and
[to] see that every child receives the benefit of it. . . . Let the
law have power to enforce attendance." It is worth noting,
however, that the writers also felt that public elementary schooling should not extend beyond three hours per child each day, in

<hr />

[39]Eugene Lawrence, "The First Century of the Republic: Educational
Progress," *Harper's New Monthly Magazine*, 51:855-856, November, 1875;
"Editor's Historical Record: Industrial Education," 46:628, March, 1873;
"Editor's Easy Chair," 50:133, December, 1874.

[40]Mott, *op. cit.*, III, 459, 465.

order to allow an additional seven or eight hours per day to those who needed to work. The editors justified this position by claiming that any schooling in excess of three hours per day was wasted effort.[41] Without any definite commitment for or against the federal assistance principle, it is difficult to assess or allocate the possible influence of *Scribner's Monthly* in this controversy. Its apparent advocacy of a nationally controlled educational policy was in direct conflict with its reluctance to impose universally what it believed to be an inadequate system. In all probability, *Scribner's* was not opposed to the more moderate federal aid proposals advanced during the 1870's, but one is led to doubt that it had any extensive influence.

Newspaper interest in the national aid issue during this period was indeed meager. Of the New York City journals, only the *Tribune* and the *Times* evidenced any concern. Both newspapers were frankly skeptical of a policy of devoting the public lands to one specific purpose, especially when that purpose was as intangible as the improvement of educational opportunity. "If both branches of Congress remain in their present temper," commented the *Tribune* during the Perce bill debate, "we shall have a little land left for the actual needs of the country, which have just now small chance in the public domain."[42] This antipathy toward applying public lands to education continued to characterize *Tribune* sentiment through the consideration of the Burnside bill. The editors, while admitting the extremities of Southern educational deficiency, did not find in the debate of 1880 any "reason for passing it (the Burnside bill) which has not been urged before, and all of them combined do not ever-come [sic] the constitutional and prudential objections to it." The people of the South, stated the *Tribune*, "should prize education enough to tax themselves for it. . . ."[43]

It is not unlikely that much of the New England attitude toward the federal aid question was reflected in the editorial

[41]"Topics of the Times; Compulsory Education," *Scribner's Monthly*, 2:95, May, 1871; "Our Educational Outlook," *Scribner's*, 4:99-100, May, 1872.
[42]New York *Tribune*, January 26, 1872; New York *Times*, February 9, 1872.
[43]New York *Tribune*, December 16, 1880; December 18, 1880.

columns of the Providence *Daily Journal*. Following a policy of general, though mild, subscription to the basic principle of federal assistance to education the *Daily Journal* registered temperate approval of the two bills. The Providence editors were concerned, however, to insure that certain elements dear to many New England hearts be firmly entrenched in the bills. Strong objections were declared to the adoption of the amendment to the Perce bill basing the distribution of moneys on illiteracy rates; the editors apparently favored a per capita distribution which would allow larger amounts to the Northeastern states. Great disturbance was indicated at the amendment to the Perce bill authorizing aid to states which maintained separate schools—the recognition of this situation by Congress, said the *Journal*, was "offensive." The Providence daily also pronounced in favor of including compulsory attendance provisions in the Perce bill and rejoiced at the rescue of the public lands from wasteful usages which such proposals were intended to accomplish. The Burnside bill debate caused the *Journal* to reiterate much of this earlier sentiment, but in 1880 some concern was evidenced that aid to schools be temporary and not such as to set a permanent precedent. Concern for New England interests was again made manifest in the plea for "a judicious, if not a judicial regard for the sections of the country which are to pay the most and receive the least."[44]

For the nation as a whole, newspaper comment upon the federal aid question during the 1870's was sparse. The Hoar bill had aroused more journalistic interest than either of the two public land bills, despite the fact that it had not even come up for a vote in Congress. It is true that the newspapers generally, when discussing education as a national issue, were primarily concerned with the question of sectarian "influences"—an issue which doubtless carried a more sensational flavor. It was the rare newspaper which even reported upon the consideration of these measures in Congress. Acute editorial concern for the federal aid issue was yet to come.

[44]Providence *Daily Journal*, February 8, 9, 12, 1872; December 18, 1880.

CONGRESSIONAL ACTION ON FEDERAL AID
TO EDUCATIONAL PROPOSALS 1872-1880

The Perce Bill[45]

The Perce bill to apply the proceeds of public land sales to education was of considerable significance for several reasons. First, it introduced the concept of devoting the public domain to common school education. Second, the consideration of this proposal served to crystallize Congressional sentiment with regard to the basic issue of federal aid and to sharpen markedly the political alignments on this issue. Third, no more able Congressional debate on the relation of the Federal Government to education had yet been held, nor was its equal to occur until 1884. And fourth, the Perce bill was the last proposal dealing with federal aid to the common schools to receive serious consideration on the floor of the House of Representatives until the Curtis-Tillman bill in 1925.

Although the final vote by which the Perce bill was passed evidenced a not inconsiderable crossing of party lines, the debate itself proceeded according to strict party alignments. The fight for the bill was carried on exclusively by the Republican representatives, while only Democratic members of the House engaged actively in opposition. Much of what had been presented in defense of and attack upon the Hoar bill reappeared in the Perce bill debate. The same Constitutional authority was submitted, the essentiality of universal education for the preservation of democracy was proclaimed, and similar references to almost unanimous support from the educational profession were made by the bill's proponents. The opposition reiterated the accusations of unconstitutionality, usurpation of states' rights, and centralization, found this simply a redesigned Hoar bill ("The old cat disguised in the meal bag"), and protested anew that this measure was essentially one part of a Republican-New England plot to increase and maintain control over the entire national life.

[45]For the entire debate on the Perce bill, see the *Congressional Globe*, 42:2, 396; 535-536; 565-570, 592-594, 691, 788-801, 851-863, 881-882; Appendix: 18-19, 39-40.

New arguments were ably presented, however, by both sides. The Republican advocates pointed to the precedents in Congressional history which supported a policy of devoting the public lands to education. From the same body of precedent, they could adduce the necessity for some degree of federal supervision over federal grants; while the aim of the measure was "only to stimulate and assist," stated Perce, "all grants should contain the power to coerce that application of the thing granted to the purpose intended." It was advanced that a *permanent* stimulus to local educational efforts was essential and that the returns from land sales, though small, would suffice for this purpose as had the money made available to the South by the Peabody bequest. There arose at this point some intra-party disagreement due to the belief of many Republicans that the need was urgent and immediate, and that Congress should allocate all, not a part, of the land sale proceeds to education outright. As passed, the bill retained the fund idea. Hoar answered the opposition's plea for recognition of states' rights by maintaining that education was the surest guarantor of those rights. "So far as the people are educated, just so far the functions and the necessities of government recede and disappear, thus rendering unnecessary the appeals to the central power which constitute the pretext of its interference." Doubtless of no little importance, though not a strictly educational consideration, was the expression of need for conservation of the public lands; the proponents maintained that no purpose to which the lands might be devoted was so worthy.

In addition to those considerations already mentioned, the opposition attacked the Perce proposal as ridiculous, in that it offered amounts of money so inconsequential as to be of no help whatsoever. (Estimates of the annual return to the states from such a fund were placed by one opposition representative at $6 to $8 per school district, and by another at $1\frac{1}{2}$ cents per child). Others maintained that the income from land sales from year to year was extremely variable and that school systems would be unable to rely upon definite amounts. Considerable concern was evidenced that this measure would ultimately mean mixed

schools for the South (this was denied by the sponsors of the
bill, who held that such arrangements were left to the states),
but an amendment eliminated that fear. The opponents of the
bill argued that pressure for such legislation was totally lacking
and that, in fact, there were other interests whose claims to
some share of the income from public lands were as valid as that
of education. While many of the Democrats who disapproved
of the Perce bill claimed that they would favor outright grants-
in-aid, with no federal controls, to needy states for educational
improvements, there were no doubt many others who felt considerable sympathy with Representative McIntyre of Georgia
when he protested: "Why, sir, this Committee on Education
and Labor is . . . nothing in the world but a sort of fungus or
excrescence that has grown upon the body politic within the
last few years. It was not known when Webster and his contemporaries were in the Congress. . . . When great men who
once occupied places in Congress have failed to bring forward
such measures as this, I feel that it is too late at this day for us to
do it; and I say that this excrescence ought to have applied to it
the surgical knife of legislation and be cut off."

After five full days of debate, in which the only Southern representatives to argue *for* the measure were two Republicans
from Mississippi, the Perce bill was brought to a vote in the
House on February 8, 1872. The measure was passed by a vote
of 117 Yeas to 98 Nays. The narrowness of this margin of vic-
tory is explained to some extent by two factors: (1) twenty
Republicans refused to follow the party and joined the Democratic opposition, and (2) the affirmative vote included twenty-
seven Republican representatives of Southern states. It is not
unlikely that, had the Southern states been free of the political
controls of reconstruction regimes, twenty-seven additional
Democrats, enough to defeat the measure, would have voted
with the opposition. Analysis of the vote indicates that of 117
Yeas only thirty-five represented the old South—the states the
measure was intended to benefit the most—and of these fourteen
were the votes of post-war immigrants from the North. Twelve
Democrats, nine of them from the North, voted with the Re-

publican majority while the twenty bolting Republicans represented states in the Middle and Far West and the Middle-
eastern seaboard. Regionally, the alignment was as follows:

	Pro	Con
New England	20	3
Middle Atlantic seaboard	24	25
Middle West	37	25
Far West	1	4
South	35	41

Thus, New England is disclosed as substantially unanimously
in favor of the measure, while the votes of Far-West representatives indicate the presence of hostility toward the proposal
in that area. The chief conclusion to be drawn from the votes
of the remaining sections, as at least a partial reflection of general public opinion, is that anything but unanimity was prevalent.

The Burnside Bill[46]

The debate in December, 1880 on the Burnside bill was neither as extensive (it lasted but three days) nor as able and thorough as that on the Perce bill. Its chief significance lies in two
features: (1) it was the first debate upon any educational, thus
any federal aid to education, measure in the Senate since the
establishment of the Bureau of Education in 1867, and (2) the
concern of the Senators revolved largely around considerations
of how best to support education rather than the question of the
constitutionality of such support.

The minor variations from the Perce bill in this measure have
been noted earlier in this chapter. The essential similarity of the
two bills meant that many of the same arguments were advanced
in its defense, as well as in the attack upon it. The usual cita-
tions of constitutional authority and the customary denials of
such authority were put forward in this debate, but these seemed
to have appeared of less consequence to the Senate than had
heretofore been true in the House. The items in the Burnside

[46]For the entire debate on the Burnside bill, see the *Congressional Record*,
46:1, 147; 46:3, 147-154, 180-185, 213-229, 1908.

bill which called forth the most vigorous controversy were those which assigned one-third of the moneys to the land-grant colleges (see page 15) and which placed the proceeds of land sales in a permanent educational fund. Both were, in effect, criticized together by many who supported the bill in principle as well as by those who were unalterably opposed to its passage. It was advanced that the entire income from land sales ought to be granted outright for educational assistance; the interest on the fund, it was claimed, would be "insignificant" and utterly inadequate to the urgent demands of the times. "We do not owe posterity anything," said Senator Ingalls of Kansas, "posterity will take care of itself." To this, the bill's sponsors replied that a permanent education fund was essential, both as a token of faith from Congress to the needy states and as inaugurating a precedent by which it was hoped increased Congressional appropriations would be stimulated in the future. Senator Morrill of Vermont strenuously objected to the idea of outright grants, expressing "regret" at the "effort . . . to reduce this great measure to the dimensions of merely an annual appropriation." To the suggestion that the allocation to the land-grant colleges of one-third of the income from the fund be eliminated, the proponents maintained that without such a provision the bill could not be passed. Apparently, the sentiment favorable to increased support of these colleges had reached considerable proportions. It was also maintained that such support was essential in order to provide for the training of the teachers who were to man the common schools.

The Burnside bill was passed on December 17, 1880, by a vote of 41 Yeas to 6 Nays. All six of the opposition voters were Democrats, four from the South and two from Indiana. Twenty-two Republicans and nineteen Democrats made up the affirmative vote, and all sections were represented. In contrast to the Perce bill vote in the House, the South, by this time almost completely returned to Democratic control, was almost solid in its support of the measure. Southern Democrats had joined Northern Republicans in leading the campaign for federal aid to common schools. Never again, however, was so decided a favorable vote to be achieved. And, with the Senate's passage of the Burnside bill, there began what became a ceaseless campaign of obstruction in the House of Representatives, for the Burnside bill was the first of many federal aid measures to be passed by the Senate and subsequently lost in the files of House committees or the intricacies of House parliamentary procedures.

THE 1870'S AS A STAGE IN THE STRUGGLE TO OBTAIN FEDERAL AID FOR COMMON SCHOOLS: SUMMARY

1. While the 1870's was a decade of relative Congressional inactivity on the matter of assistance to education, it saw the advancement, though not the enactment, of a new departure in federal aid legislation. This was the policy of devoting the proceeds of public land sales to common school education, a procedure for which there was considerable precedent.

2. Though no law was enacted, a new precedent was inaugurated, that of allowing the use of federal funds in states which maintained separate school systems for the different races.

3. Increasing concern about the issue of federal assistance to education was manifested by the educational profession, but educators were totally unable to unite on a policy of support or rejection.

4. The Catholic Church, in reaffirming its belief in the essential immorality of the public school system, was utterly unable to subscribe to federal aid in any form. The Church repeated its insistence that, if such a program were enacted, private denominational schools must share in the moneys distributed.

5. Organized farmer, labor, and business groups—due to insufficient organization, preoccupation with more immediate concerns, or indifference—took no stands on the matter of federal aid to education.

6. Certain of the more influential magazines began to show an interest in the federal aid question and to present definite views with regard to it. Newspapers, in general, continued to ignore the matter.

7. In the South, the decade was characterized by increasing awareness of that region's educational problem and the possibility of obtaining federal assistance to meet that problem. Other sections, particularly the Far West, evidenced varying degrees of indifference to the attempts to present educational delinquency as a national concern.

8. The 1870's was featured by definite declarations and manifestations of party policy regarding federal aid to education. In general, Republican party policy and actions favored enactment of federal aid measures, while Democratic party statements and voting records opposed such legislation. The vote in the Senate on the Burnside bill was evidence of a reinterpretation of policy on the part of the Democratic party—for a time, regional necessity was to outweigh political tradition.

9. The Perce bill was the last proposal of federal aid to common schools to be seriously considered by the House of Representatives for over half a century.

10. The Burnside bill was the first proposal of federal assistance to common schools to be seriously considered by the Senate. While this bill marked the beginning of a new decade of unprecedented, and to date unequaled, activity and concern on the part of Congress for the federal aid issue, the deliberations of the 1880's revolved around a new and untried principle in the realm of federal participation in education. It is this new approach and the forces surrounding its introduction and consideration that the two succeeding chapters will consider.

· V ·

THE ATTEMPTS TO AID COMMON SCHOOLS BY DIRECT APPROPRIATION OF MONEY 1882-1890: THE BLAIR BILL: INTRODUCTION, PUBLIC PRESSURE, AND RESPONSE

THE PROPOSALS: THEIR PROVISIONS

Introductory Proposals

THE decade of the 1880's, as the final climactic phase of this first struggle to enact federal legislation to aid common schools, was ushered in by the last important proposal to supply such aid through the use of the proceeds of public lands sales. Never since that time has this method been seriously considered. A totally new departure in federal aid legislation characterized the period 1880 to 1890, one which, in many respects, established that period as the real beginning of current activity in this area. For in 1882, and especially in the years 1884 to 1890, there were introduced into Congress proposals of federal assistance based upon the direct appropriation of money to states from the national treasury. The principles and arguments upon which these plans were based, the bases of opposition to them, and the over-all tenor of public response and reaction then evidenced carry profound implications for the effective meeting of a contemporary situation which in very large measure is essentially similar.

The bill which, with some variations, occupied the Senate almost continuously from 1884 to 1890 was first presented to that body by Senator Henry W. Blair of New Hampshire in June, 1882. It did not gain recognition and was not considered, however, until after its reintroduction in 1884. By that time, certain other legislative suggestions had been brought before Congress, which, though their examination had been cursory at best, had served to point the direction in which subsequent proposals were likely to move. The first of these was contained in a bill offered by Senator Logan of Illinois, which provided for the appropriation to education of "the entire income derived from the internal-revenue taxes on the manufacture and sale of distilled spirits."[1] While this was, basically, a scheme which substituted certain specific federal revenues for the proceeds of public land sales, it introduced the element of direct appropriation to education of moneys raised by taxation. (This bill is significant, too, as the first to reach the floor of either house which required states and territories to enact compulsory school attendance laws as a condition of receiving federal aid). Subsequently, two measures were presented to the House of Representatives— the Updegraff bill in 1882[2] and the Sherwin bill in 1883[3]—which provided that a *temporary direct* appropriation of $10,000,000 annually for five years be made from the national treasury "to aid in the support of free common-schools." A transition was thus accomplished from proposals embracing the utilization of particular sources of government revenue to measures based upon direct appropriation out of the general fund. Furthermore, these plans were evidence that an idea of temporary aid to meet a current emergency had supplanted the earlier reliance upon permanent allocations and long-term commitments. It was in this developing framework that the Blair bill was first presented and examined.

The Blair Bills: Their Provisions[4]

Senator Blair presented his bill "to aid in the establishment and temporary support of common schools" five times during the 1880's. Extensive debate and Senate action followed all

[1]*Congressional Record*, 47:1, 1950.
[2]*Ibid.*, 47:1, 6534.
[3]*Ibid.*, 47:2, 1203-04, 3257.
[4]For complete texts of the Blair bill, see *Congressional Record*, 47:1, 4833 (1882), 48:1, 1999 (1884), 49:1, 1239 (1886).

but the first presentation in 1882; the bill was passed by the Senate in 1884, 1886, and 1888; it failed of passage in 1890. The bill as passed in 1884 was substantially different from that which had been introduced two years before, but few significant changes were made in the measure after 1884.

The bill as originally introduced provided that for ten years after its passage, annual appropriations from the national treasury to the states were to be made, beginning with an appropriation of $15,000,000 the first year. Each subsequent appropriation was to be reduced by $1,000,000; after the tenth such grant the appropriations were to cease. As passed by the Senate in 1884 and thereafter, the method of appropriation was revised, for reasons which will be noted later. The approved scheme provided for an ascending-descending scale of appropriations over a period of eight years: $7,000,000 the first year, $10,000,000 the second year, $15,000,000 the third year, $13,000,000 the fourth year, $11,000,000 the fifth year, $9,000,000 the sixth year, $7,000,000 the seventh year, and $5,000,000 the eighth year— a total of $77,000,000. The Senate in 1886 made one further change in the amount of money involved in these bills by providing that, during the first year, an additional $2,000,000 was to be made available for the building of schoolhouses. (This additional section provided that such schoolhouses as were built with these funds were to conform to plans drawn by the Bureau of Education and that in no case would more than $150 or one-half the cost of construction, whichever was lower, be contributed toward such construction by this fund). The two succeeding Blair bills retained this feature.

The manner in which this money was to be appropriated and distributed was established by the bill as it passed the Senate in 1884. Section 2 of that and the three succeeding bills provided "That such money shall annually be divided among and paid out in the several States and Territories in that proportion which the whole number of persons in each who, being of the age of 10 years and over, can not write, bears to the whole number of such persons in the United States; such computations shall be made according to the census of 1880." In 1886, there was added the stipulation that the returns of the census of 1890 should be utilized whenever they became available. Section 14 further required that states and territories were to "distribute the moneys raised for common school purposes equally for the education of all the children, without distinction of race or color"; this proviso applied both to the moneys raised locally by states or communities and to the grants received from the Federal Government. Thus, where separate schools for white and Negro children were maintained, support was to be apportioned between them on the basis of the proportion that each group bore to the other.

Definite conditions were assigned to the states, non-fulfillment of which constituted disqualification from the benefits of the act, as follows:

1. Each state was required to provide "by law a system of free common schools for all of its children of school age, without distinction of race or color, either in the raising or distributing of school revenues or in the school facilities provided."

2. Each state governor was required to submit to the Secretary of the Interior reports descriptive of the common school system operative in his state, dealing with such matters as attendance, number of schools, moneys raised and expended, and evidences of non-discrimination.

3. The curriculum in the schools to be supported or established with federal funds was to include "the art of reading, writing, and speaking the English language, arithmetic, geography, history of the United States, and such other branches of useful knowledge as may be taught under local laws. . . ." The territories were authorized to apply this money to "industrial" (i.e. agriculture and mechanic arts) as well as common schools.

4. No portion of the grants was to be spent for schoolhouse rental or construction, except as provided by the special authorization for the first year of the operation of the act.

5. The "moneys distributed under the provisions of this act shall be used only for common schools, not sectarian in character, in the . . . several States, and only for common or indus-

trial schools in Territories, in such way as to provide, as near as may be, for the equalization of school privileges to all the children of school age. . . ."

The bill as originally introduced in 1882 and again in 1884 provided that for the first three years of the operation of the act the states were to spend from their own revenues on education a sum one-third as large as the federal grants they received. For the remaining five years, the states were required to spend on education an amount equaling the total of federal grants each received. It was argued that, at the outset, it would be impossible for many Southern states to match the federal grants. As passed in 1884, however, the bill made mandatory from the start the matching principle—"it is hereby provided that no greater part of the money appropriated under this act shall be paid out to any State or Territory in any one year than the sum expended out of its own revenues or out of moneys raised under its authority in the preceding year for the maintenance of common schools. . . ." This feature remained unchanged throughout all subsequent considerations of the Blair bill.

It has been noted that one of the conditions laid upon each state was the provision by law of a "system of free common schools for all of its children of school age," with no distinction of race or color in the raising or distribution of school funds. Following the practice inaugurated by the Perce bill, a proviso to the effect that "separate schools for white and colored children shall not be considered a violation of this condition" was included in all versions of the bill. Southern senators considered such a clarification essential and Northern supporters of the bill rightly concluded that, without such a proviso, there was small hope of the bill's passage.

In only one respect did the Blair bills grant discretionary authority over the use of the federal funds to the states. This was in the area of teacher training. Many senators recognized that one of the basic problems to be faced was the woefully inadequate supply of properly trained teachers for the common schools and questioned the practicability of appropriating money to the schools without providing for the personnel who were to staff them. Thus, in each of the bills as presented and as passed by the Senate, it was provided that as much as one-tenth of the money apportioned to a state might be used, in any way the state saw fit, to promote the training of common school teachers. The language of the bill indicated that normal schools or other teacher training institutions might thus be supported or that scholarships might be created to enable "competent and suitable persons" to train for the teaching profession.

The administrative machinery for this system of federal grants was set forth in some detail. Upon the basis of the state reports mentioned earlier, the Secretary of the Interior was authorized to "certify" to the Secretary of the Treasury the eligible states. This, of course, meant that it was the responsibility of the Commissioner of Education in turn—who was made the agent of the Secretary of the Interior in administering the act—to indicate to that official (his superior) those states and territories which had qualified for aid. The Secretary of the Treasury then was required to pay the apportioned amounts to "such officers as shall be authorized by the laws of the respective States and Territories to receive the same," that is, to state officials, who were responsible for using the money in accordance with the provisions of the bill. Finally, the Secretary of the Interior was required to report annually to Congress upon the operation of this legislation, and states or territories were granted the right of an appeal directly to Congress over adverse decisions by that Secretary or the Commissioner of Education.

To recapitulate, the following were probably the most significant of the provisions of the Blair bills as they underwent Congressional and public scrutiny over a period of eight years:

1. A system of direct monetary federal aid, temporary in character, increasing in amount for three years, decreasing for five years.
2. A plan of distribution based upon the rates of illiteracy of persons over ten years of age.
3. Appropriations whose sizes were governed by the extent of local expenditures for education—i.e. the "matching" principle.

4. A system of aid to public common schools only, excluding denominational schools from the benefits of the act, designed in so far as possible to equalize educational opportunities.

5. Grants to be administered by state and local officials within a framework of certain general federal requirements and restrictions.

PUBLIC PRESSURE WITH REGARD TO FEDERAL AID TO COMMON SCHOOL EDUCATION

That the introduction of the Blair bills and the prospect of immediate financial aid to common school education from the federal treasury aroused widespread public interest is undeniable. No previous educational legislation had elicited anything remotely comparable to the volume of public demand for Congressional action as was stimulated by these proposals during the 1880's. The accompanying chart attempts to indicate numerically the dimensions of this pressure upon Congress throughout the ten-year period in which the Blair bills were under consideration. These data are based upon the registration of petitions and memorials contained in the *Congressional Record* for the period extending from the first session of the Forty-seventh Congress (December, 1881 to August, 1882) through the second session of the Fifty-first Congress (December, 1890 to March, 1891).[5]

It is apparent at first glance that, regardless of region, the vast majority of these petitions or memorials originated with groups of "citizens"—unorganized (except locally), separate, representative bodies of people who were deeply concerned with the problem of educational improvement. While the largest number of these "citizen" petitions was sent from the South, and the volume of Southern petitions remained somewhat more

[5]For registry of petitions, see *Congressional Record*, indices, as follows: 47:2, 57; 48:1, 147; 48:2, 63; 49:1, 191-2; 49:2, 59; 50:1, 253; 51:1, 231; 51:2, 1387. For 47:1, no index is available, hence petitions from that session are found throughout the *Record*; for 50:2, the index records no petitions dealing with federal aid to education.

PETITIONS TO CONGRESS REQUESTING THE ENACTMENT OF LEGISLATION GRANTING AID TO THE COMMON SCHOOLS—1881 TO 1891

Sources	Sessions of Congress in Which Received									
	1881 -82 47:1	1882 -83 47:2	1883 -84 48:1	1884 -85 48:2	1885 -86 49:1	1886 -87 49:2	1887 -88 50:1	1888 -89 50:2	1889 -90 51:1	1890 -91 51:2
SOUTH										
Citizens	194	9	105	11	80	40	106		38	
State governments	3	7	2		5		1			
Public educational organizations	1	1	7	6	16	1				
Business organizations										
College faculties		10								
Religious groups			1		1	2	1		1	
Labor organizations					1					
Reform group (WCTU)						8	1			
	198	27	115	17	103	51	109		39	
NORTHEAST										
Citizens	22	1	2	5	9	151	221		34	
State governments	3						2			
Public educational organizations	2					1	1		1	
Business organizations	1		1						6	
College faculties	1	3								
Religious groups			3						1	
Labor organizations										
Reform group (WCTU)						7	2			
	29	4	6	5	9	159	226		42	
MIDDLE WEST										
Citizens	3	1	3	1	3	102	146		12	
State governments	1									
Public educational organizations	1	2	1		3					
Business organizations										
College faculties	1									
Religious groups										
Labor organizations										
Reform group (WCTU)						21				
	6	3	4	1	6	123	146		12	
FAR WEST										
Citizens	3		2			14	34		2	
State governments		1								
Public educational organizations		1		1						
Business organizations										
College faculties										
Religious groups										
Labor organizations										
Reform group (WCTU)										
	3	2	2	1		14	34		2	
NATIONAL ORGANIZATIONS										
Educational		4	1							
Religious			1				1		1	
Labor							1		2	
Miscellaneous						1	7		8	
		4	2			1	9		11	
GRAND TOTAL	236	40	129	24	119	347	524	*		1*

*For the Session 50:2, no petitions on this subject were recorded; for the Session 51:2, only one such petition was registered in the *Congressional Record*, from a "citizens'" group, unidentified as to region.

constant until the end of the decade, there is abundant evidence
to show that the public of other regions had also been aroused
to this issue. By 1887, both the Northeast and the Middle West,
to judge from the number of petitions to Congress, had become
keenly interested in federal aid; even the Far West apparently
grew somewhat less indifferent toward the end of the decade.
It is clear, however, that interest in the Blair bills diminished as
distance from the South increased; thus it was in New England
and the Middle Atlantic states that the largest degree of public
interest, outside the South itself, was to be found, while the Far-
Western states evidenced only slight concern.

It is apparent, too, that a decided diminution in the volume of
pressure upon Congress appeared after 1888. This reduced demand, especially from the South, supported the contentions of
those who, in the late 1880's, were arguing that Southern self-
help had begun to solve the educational problem and therefore
federal funds were no longer needed. There is evidence here to
indicate that the desire on the part of Southerners for federal
assistance had noticeably decreased by 1890.

Organizational pressures upon Congress in behalf of federal
aid to education increased during the 1880's, but that increase
cannot be considered marked. Some organizations were far
more active in the struggle over support for common schools
than the presence or absence of petitions to Congress would indicate. This was especially true of certain of the religious denominations, many of which failed to memorialize Congress
formally but were quite active in publicizing their views in the
ecclesiastical press. Similarly, the registry of petitions in Congress is not a true index of the extreme concern of the educational profession.

For some associations, however, the petitions and memorials
constituted the major expression of sentiment. Thus, it is clear
that many Southern educational groups, both associations of
teachers and administrative bodies like the superintendents of
schools of Virginia, consistently requested federal support, while
educational organizations of other regions were, like the public
generally, much less concerned. Certain university and college

faculties, especially those of small private institutions in the South, expressed some interest. Occasionally, the faculty of a Northern private college or state university joined in the demand for some sort of federal aid. The disinterest of farmer and business groups can be noted in the almost complete absence of petitions from those sources.

Finally, there was a decided lack of pressure on anything approximating a national scale. Memorials from the National Education Association were continuous until 1890, at which time they abruptly ceased. The only other national organization which carried on a vigorous campaign of petitions to Congress for the Blair bill or similar legislation was the Women's Christian Temperance Union, which, though founded in 1874, did not become active in the battle for federal aid until 1886. For the rest of the decade, petitions from national and local headquarters of the Women's Christian Temperance Union were constantly placed before Congress. That this organization had already reached a position of considerable influence is evidenced by the fact that, during the first session of the Forty-ninth Congress, when the Blair bill controversy was at its height, approximately 425 petitions demanding "scientific temperance instruction in schools under control of the Federal Government" were received by the Congress. During that session, only 119 petitions relative to the federal aid issue were received.

It was not until the Blair bill was before the Senate for the fourth and last time in 1890 that any petitions opposing the bill were registered in the *Congressional Record*. During this session (51:1) three such memorials were received, all of which originated with groups of citizens in the Middle West. Throughout the 1880's, occasional statements had been recorded which expressed opposition to any appropriation of federal funds for the benefit of schools under sectarian control. Conceivably, these might be construed as containing an element of hostility to federal aid generally, in so far as federal funds might have been used, in rare instances (i.e. in Utah, with schools under Mormon control, or in New Mexico, where most schools were Catholic in orientation), to support public schools under denominational influence. Suffice it to say, however, that the officially registered demands upon Congress relative to federal aid were so preponderantly in favor of such aid as to make the opposition negligible. The opponents of the Blair bill operated with great effectiveness in other channels.

PUBLIC RESPONSE TO THE BLAIR BILL

There can be no general characterization of the public response to the bill proposed by Senator Blair. The educational profession, the press, and most churches were hopelessly divided in their attitudes toward this plan; only in rare instances can the official pronouncements of any group or organization on this issue be considered representative of a substantial majority of its membership. Certain segments of society, notably the educators, were far more active and vocal than others, while groups less directly concerned were, in some instances, apparently completely disinterested. This section first examines the positions of those social elements which were least active. Then, turning to those groups whose behavior must have been instrumental in producing the extensive Congressional interest for which the Blair bill has been acclaimed, there is presented an analysis of the forces which brought about its ultimate defeat. As an agent of synthesis, the press is considered last, though, as will be emphasized, its influence was by no means the least of the factors which determined the outcome of this legislative struggle.

The National Farmers' Alliance

Evidence that organized agriculture was actively interested in the question of federal aid to education during the 1880's is very meager, but there were indications that farmers were in sympathy with attempts to improve educational conditions. The National Farmers' Alliance and Cooperative Union of America, representing a combination of farmers' clubs and associations in Southern states, and the Northern Farmers' Alliance, which came to dominate the agricultural forces of the Northcentral and Midwestern states, a combination of which became the nu-

cleus of the Populist party formed in 1892, were committed to
the support of public education.

The Northern Alliance had specified in its original Declaration
of Purposes a resolve "To labor for the education of the agricultural classes in the science of economical government in a
strictly non-partisan spirit."[6] Like the Grange in the 1870's,
however, the Northern farmers apparently conceived of the educational problem as one which did not concern the Federal
Government and as requiring internal modification rather than
external support or direction. It is difficult to deduce energetic
concern for the promotion of federal aid from statements such
as the following, adopted by the Alliance of the North in 1888:
"Resolved, That we believe in so amending the Public School
System that the education of our children shall be of practical
help to them in after life. . . . Our country needs an educational
system, based on moral, manual and intellectual training that in-
culcates the essential dignity and necessity of honest labor."[7]

The Southern Farmers' Alliance was doubtless more acutely
aware of serious educational deficiencies, and, while not pro-
nouncing itself definitely in favor of federal aid legislation, established from its inception a sympathetic position. At its first
convention in 1887, the Southern Alliance published a series of
"Demands" upon Congress among which appeared the statement
"That as upon the intelligence of the people depend the stability
and perpetuity of our own free government, we demand for the
masses a well-regulated system of industrial and agricultural education."[8] While interest in a kind of education peculiarly bene-
ficial to farmers and industrial workers loomed largest, the recognition that education and republican institutions were inter-
dependent and the mere fact that such a demand was made of
the national Congress indicate the existence of a certain sympathy with some form of national activity in educational affairs.
There is evidence, however, that some Southern farmers were
definitely opposed to the Blair bill. One of the few petitions to

[6]E. A. Allen, *Labor and Capital*, 395.
[7]*Ibid.*, 399.
[8]W. A. Dunning, *The Farmers' Alliance History and Agricultural Digest*, 76.

Congress requesting the defeat of that legislation was sent in 1888 by the Agricultural Wheel of Centre Hill, Arkansas, an organization which joined forces with the Alliance one year later.[9]

Organized farmers had not yet become a positive factor in the struggle for national educational legislation. Preoccupation with more immediate economic concerns and the traditional feeling, stronger perhaps among farmers than with other groups, that education was a strictly local affair resulted in an indifference to proposals for the improvement of public education through federal efforts. No platforms of the Populist party made any mention of education, a fact which, while not connoting antagonism to the principle of federal assistance for education, strongly suggests that throughout this period such policies were not considered among the vital interests of farmers.

Organized Labor

While the early 1880's constituted a period of relative economic prosperity, producing, according to Curoe, little concern on the part of organized labor for anything other than improved working conditions, this decade was characterized by a decided intensification of union interest in educational affairs. The Knights of Labor, which in the 1870's had been inactive with regard to national educational developments, apparently took the lead among labor organizations in supporting the Blair bill. In 1886, the Knights resolved unequivocally that "the cause of education would be promoted by the passage of the Blair educational bill"[10] and its failure to pass the Forty-ninth Congress elicited strong censure from the organization, which expressed particular concern at the Congressional indifference to Southern distress. Throughout the 1880's, the Knights of Labor retained an established lobby in Washington which, notes Curoe, "kept close watch upon the Blair Education Bill."[11] Repeatedly, the Knights petitioned Congress in behalf of federal aid and sent delegations to Washington to testify in its support.

[9]*Congressional Record*, 50:1, 2985.
[10]Henry W. Blair (comp.), *The Education Bill*, cover page 3.
[11]Philip R. V. Curoe, *Educational Attitudes and Policies of Organized Labor in the United States*, 85-86.

The interest in education which was to characterize the American Federation of Labor was foreshadowed to some extent by the published sentiments of one of its predecessors, the Federation of Organized Trades and Labor Unions of the United States. Its original platform, adopted in 1881, in a statement immediately following demands for the legal recognition of trade unions, pronounced complete subscription to a policy of legally enforced compulsory education.[12] Dependence upon action through state rather than national government was still considered most effective, as evidenced by the following from this organization's annual report in 1884: "While National legislation should not be overlooked, it is nevertheless a fact that the State legislatures form the most favorable point of attack and most of the legislative reforms we advocate must be obtained through this medium."[13]

Curoe summarizes the position of the American Federation of Labor by noting that it "has consistently worked for a larger measure of federal participation in education. . . . [There has been] no instance in the official records of the American Federation of Labor where a move towards greater federal participation in education has been opposed. . . . [But] its policy has been opposed to federal dictation or mandatory legislation; it has stood rather for federal encouragement."[14] Support of the Blair bill was a factor in the Federation's public policy from its establishment in 1886 through 1890, although support of federal aid was in fact considered to be one element in the achievement of a greater end—universal compulsory education. Resolutions favoring federal participation in education were adopted regularly without debate, but only in 1887 and 1889 did these include specific approval of the Blair bill itself. The reasons advanced for such support are noteworthy as indicating the orientation of labor thought at the time. The Blair bill was deemed essential in view of (1) the need for a citizenry familiar with the operation of the American governmental system, and (2)

[12]Federation of Organized Trades and Labor Unions of the United States, *Annual Report*, 1881, iii.

[13]*Ibid., 1884*, 20.

[14]Curoe, *op. cit.*, 126-130.

the belief that no social reform was possible without improved public education.[15] While sectional needs apparently did not loom large in the councils of labor, the Federation favored "the greatest liberality . . . by the United States and state Governments to further and advance the cause of the education of the masses."[16]

The Blair bill was the only measure proposing federal aid to non-vocational education actively favored by the American Federation of Labor before 1919, but its continuous sympathy with such legislation must be re-emphasized. As indicated earlier, extensive interest on the part of organized labor in such legislation appeared only after the affiliation of teachers with the labor movement, but the tacit support of organized labor has always served to lend strength to any attempt to provide increased federal assistance for public education.

Organized Business

Only isolated evidences of interest on the part of organized business interests in the enactment of national educational legislation appeared during the 1880's. Such specific indications as did appear, almost exclusively in the form of petitions to Congress, were all of a favorable tenor—no group of consequence in the realm of business went on record as opposing such a program. There were a few pronouncements on other matters of concern to business which might be construed to imply opposition to federal aid to education, but, in general, this was an area in which business leaders had neither interest nor familiarity.

An exception to this characterization was the Union League Club of New York City, an organization of business and professional men with Republican allegiance, which undertook, with considerable vigor, to improve the conditions of education both locally and nationally. While most of its efforts in this regard were confined to operations within the city or state systems, the Union League Club was among the most consistent of the

---

[15]*Report of the Proceedings of the Second Annual Session of the American Federation of Labor, 1887*, 29-30.
[16]American Federation of Labor, *Labor and Education*, 8.

petitioners for federal aid legislation. Its resolutions of 1882, for example, state that the Club "heartily approves of the scope and object" of the Blair bill and respectfully requests its enactment by the Congress.[17] Equally regular, however, was this group's unalterable opposition to the use of public funds for the support of denominationally controlled schools, labeling such demands "the insidious attack upon our common-school system."[18] Both positions were forcefully summarized by one of the founders and most influential leaders of the Union League Club, John Jay, grandson of the first Chief Justice of the United States, lawyer, onetime minister to Austria, and ubiquitous public servant. As a prominent Republican and constant defender of the public schools, Jay considered the Blair bill absolutely essential to Southern recovery. Of its constitutionality he held no doubts whatever—those who would deny such aid on grounds of unconstitutionality, he declared, were arguing that there must be one interpretation for the North and "another by which the South will be made to bear alone" the development of free public education. Jay considered the measure to be even more essential to the nation as a whole. He maintained that "the chief opponents of [federal aid], are those who desire the destruction of the common school system as the bulwark of the republic and of its civil and religious freedom." Without such aid, ignorance and illiteracy "will convert the suffrage itself into the most dangerous weapon with which the foes of American liberty, who are now so desperately attacking our common school system, can undermine our press and our institutions, and overthrow our civil and religious freedom."[19]

The Union League Club was joined in its petitions to Congress by the Boston Chamber of Commerce and Board of Trade; otherwise, business associations appear to have been altogether silent on educational affairs in general. That some business groups might have opposed the Blair bill had its passage in the House of Representatives appeared possible seems a valid infer-

[17]*Congressional Record*, 47:1, 1230.
[18]*The Union League Club of New York*, 55.
[19]John Jay, "The Nation and the Schools"; letter to the New York *Tribune*, published February 20, 1888.

ence. The records of the conventions of the American Bankers' Association from 1875 through 1890 reveal very little concern with social questions of any nature. The presence of continued pleas for the removal of wartime federal taxes upon banking institutions, leaving them to be taxed by state and local agencies only, suggests that legislation which involved increased federal expenditure or expanded federal powers would have been disapproved.[20] Similarly, *Railway Age,* the organ of the American railroads, regularly campaigned against government regulation in the field of transportation—consistency would seem to demand a negative reaction here as well to proposals of federal participation in local activities, regardless of their nature.

As it was in the case of organized labor, so for business this was a period in which extensive interest in social programs of this character was not to be expected. Only as business interests were definitely and directly affected did concern for the actions of the Federal Government arise. Even the cry of the 1870's that federal aid legislation would serve to protect the public lands from the exploitations of industry had failed to provoke a response from business leaders. Participation in what Parrington calls the "Great Barbecue" left little time or energy for social reform.

The Grand Army of the Republic

Probably the single most effective and influential pressure group in the United States during this period was the organization of Union Army veterans, the Grand Army of the Republic. As such, its stand or lack of stand on the federal aid question is of some significance. The pronouncements and activities of the Grand Army of the Republic throughout the 1870's and 1880's were characterized by an absence of position relative to this or any other important social issue. No concern for any aspect of education was expressed, except that every national encampment through that of 1890 passed resolutions demanding the provision by the Federal Government of educational facilities for the orphans of soldiers and sailors.

[20]American Bankers' Association, *Reports of Proceedings,* 1875 to 1889, 9.

The G. A. R.'s lone entry into educational affairs began with its expression of concern, in 1888, over the production and use of United States history textbooks which it considered objectionable as partisan or sectional interpretations. On this issue, considerable interest was maintained throughout the 1890's, but this led to no involvement in the question of federal participation in education.[21] The official G. A. R. historian explains this policy of disinterest in social affairs when he reports that, in 1887, a resolution condemning any attempt to allow statehood to Utah while Mormonism remained legal was "non-concurred in by the Encampment, for the reason that its discussion would be foreign to the work and objects of the Grand Army of the Republic."[22]

The Educational Profession

During the decade the performance of the National Education Association, which by the 1880's held a position of unquestioned pre-eminence and prestige within the profession, presents a striking and accurate reflection of the general attitude of much of the profession toward federal aid. The Association's early recognition of the problem of educational deficiency has been noted. In accordance with the tenor of legislative proposals then under consideration, the National Education Association in 1881 reaffirmed its support of the policy of devoting public lands proceeds to public education.[23] With the introduction of the Blair bill in 1882, and probably stimulated by the suggestions of John Eaton, the Commissioner of Education, the Association promptly swung its support to the principle of direct financial assistance. The National Education Association convention of 1882, in a resolution adopted unanimously by approximately one thousand educators from more than thirty states, sent to all members of Congress the following: "Resolved, That in the opinion of this Association, it is the duty of the Congress of the United States, to make a liberal appropriation from the national treasury

[21]Bessie L. Pierce, *Public Opinion and the Teaching of History*, 164 ff.

[22]Robert B. Beath, *History of the Grand Army of the Republic*, 342.

[23]*The Addresses and Journal of Proceedings of the National Educational Association, Session of the Year 1881, at Atlanta, Georgia*, 159.

for the support of the schools in the States, on the basis of illiteracy."[24]

From then until 1886, the National Education Association grew increasingly vehement in its demands for direct temporary financial support for education, especially for the schools of the South, and at nearly every session of Congress, a deputation representing the Association testified before Congressional committees, urging passage of the Blair bill. The strongest statements were the resolutions of 1884 and 1885, the former following the first passage of the Blair bill by the Senate, the latter demanding its reconsideration after the failure of the lower house to act. In 1884, the National Education Association resolved:

That the educators of the United States, in National Convention assembled, most heartily commend the recent action of the United States Senate in making a liberal appropriation of money to aid the several States in their efforts to lessen and remove the alarming illiteracy which so seriously threatens free institutions, and they most earnestly hope that this important measure may receive the early and favorable consideration of the House of Representatives.[25]

The resolution of 1885 read:

Resolved . . . that the Congress of the United States be earnestly recommended to extend such liberal pecuniary aid to the people of all the States and territories, for the purpose of aiding them, so far as the financial condition of the federal government will justify, to the end that every child in the country of school age may receive a good common school education under the respective systems of the several States.[26]

In 1887, the Association reaffirmed "with emphasis" its previous calls for financial assistance for Southern education and found the Blair bill "a fit measure to accomplish this end."[27] Resolutions of the same general tenor were adopted by the conventions of 1888 and 1889, but the language of the statements reflected a gradually increasing lack of concern for the federal aid question which was characteristic of the profession. By 1890, the National Education Association went on record in

[24]*Ibid., 1882*, x.
[25]*Ibid., 1884*, 12.
[26]*Ibid., 1885*, 20.
[27]*Ibid., 1887*, 45.

much more general terms by resolving that "a great responsibility rests upon state and society" for insuring every child moral, intellectual, and occupational training; "and that we fully approve judicious legislation and philanthropic effort directed to these ends."[28] But by 1891, after the final defeat of the Blair bill, the Association declared its satisfaction with the national, and particularly the Southern educational situation. "The Association observes with pleasure the manifest enlargement of educational activity in the Southern States of the Union. . . . With peculiar satisfaction we observe and record the fact, and congratulate our friends of the fair and sunny South upon its development."[29]

The records of the National Education Association conventions indicate that, as the resolutions requesting federal aid to education were gradually weakened and allowed to disappear, the discussions of the question in convention meetings likewise diminished. The number of papers and addresses on this issue presented to the Association constantly decreased until, by 1891, official consideration of federal aid was totally lacking. Keith and Bagley state that the National Education Association, by 1890, recognized that the lately passed Hatch Act (establishing agricultural experiment stations) and the second Morrill Act (increasing the endowments of the land-grant colleges) "constituted a first mortgage on the net proceeds of the sale of public lands," and threw its efforts into the enhancement of these measures of federal aid.[30] Thus, it appears that the Association, as the result of either a feeling that Southern education was at last on its own feet or a reluctance to continue commitments to programs of direct federal financial aid, returned to advocacy of the established practice of supporting education from land sale proceeds. It was not until 1906, and more importantly 1919, that the National Education Association resumed staunch advocacy of federal aid directly to the common schools.

Two other national bodies served to highlight the increased

[28]Ibid., 1890, 39.
[29]Ibid., 1891, 39.
[30]John A. H. Keith and William C. Bagley, The Nation and Its Schools, 116.

professional interest in the federal aid problem during the early 1880's. Though short-lived and of doubtful effect, they epitomized the sentiments of a large part of the educational profession. The first of these was the "National Education Assembly" which convened in Atlantic City in 1882 and 1883 for the avowed purpose of marshaling public opinion behind the idea of federal assistance to public education. This assemblage, described as being composed of "Christian educators and statesmen irrespective of section, Church or party," gathered together "to awaken and direct public sentiment in favor of enlarged National, State, and Church effort, for the education and elevation of our illiterate and degraded masses."[31] It was felt that this group represented, as had no other gathering, the combined strength of the major educational associations, the various Protestant denominations, and the Bureau of Education. In 1884, the secretary of this Assembly's Committee on National Education reported that the two previous conventions and the efforts which they stimulated had produced much in the form of organized pressure in favor of federal aid legislation. The report cited the following: that six thousand letters had been addressed to the nation's leading educators asking their support, that these and other efforts had produced "several thousand" petitions to Congress requesting federal assistance, which petitions contained between forty and fifty thousand signatures from twenty-three states and territories; that eight states, through their legislatures or by petitions signed by state officials, had been induced to submit similar memorials; that numerous petitions from professional associations, religious organizations, and college faculties had been stimulated. The report concluded pessimistically, however, that while this "shows that a sentiment is growing throughout the entire country . . . demanding that these things shall be done . . . the average Congressman regards it simply as the opinion of sentimental educators and philanthropists. . . ."[32]

A second, and somewhat similar, effort was made in 1883

[31]J. C. Hartzell (ed.), *Christian Educators in Council: Sixty Addresses by American Educators, National Education Assembly, August 1883*, introduction.

[32]*Ibid.*, 35.

when, on the initiative of certain Southern state governors, an Inter-State Educational Convention was held. Educational leaders, appointed by and representative of the governors, met to consider how best to meet the educational needs of the country. Although a notable gathering, it is doubtful that the efforts of this group approached the influence of the National Education Assembly. The tangible accomplishments of the Inter-State Educational Convention were confined to (1) the publication of a resolution "cordially" approving the principle of national aid but demanding exclusively state control over the use of the money and (2) the drafting of a "Bill to Establish an Educational Fund to Aid in the Support of Public Schools." The bill was significant in that, unlike the Blair bill, it provided a schedule of appropriations which granted a set sum for each illiterate person between the ages of 10 and 20, and in providing a "Board of Trustees" (consisting of the Secretary of the Interior, two Senators and two Representatives from more than one party, the Commissioner of Education, and a Treasury Department auditor) to administer the act. This proposal was then submitted to various educational leaders, governors, and college presidents for their appraisal. While it is probable that this bill, in some form, reached a Congressional committee, none of its basic provisions were brought forth on the floor of the Senate during the Blair bill debates. The Inter-State Educational Convention was symptomatic of the growing concern among educators and legislators alike, but its contribution to the pressures that were developing is hardly discernible.[33]

From other allied or quasi-educational organizations, little was heard during the 1880's relative to the Blair bill or its basic principle. One such organization did make its position clear, however, and in unequivocal language. This was the American Social Science Association which, in 1882, publicly indicated its grave concern over the degree of illiteracy and ignorance in the United States. Reasserting the faith that republican liberties are guaranteed by intelligence and convinced that the Constitution

[33]Inter-State Educational Commission on Federal Aid to Education, *Federal Aid to Education. A Bill to Provide a Fund of $65,737,290*, 3-12.

authorized federal legislation in aid of public education, this association pled for direct financial assistance on a temporary basis in the alleviation of conditions of illiteracy. It was careful to stipulate, however, that this aid be supplied "in such manner as shall not supersede or interfere with local efforts, but rather stimulate the same and render them more efficient."[34]

The efforts of state educational or teachers' associations were apparently most effective in producing petitions and memorials to be sent to Congress. As noted earlier, declarations of support for the Blair bill from such organizations reached Congress from all sections of the country. Further, and of more importance, it seems safe to conclude that a considerable portion of the petitions originating with groups of "citizens" were stimulated by the work of state and local educational associations. State educational organization publications and convention records contained numerous resolutions supporting the Blair bill, but again the Southern groups were, naturally, most keenly aware of the urgency of the need for aid.

The history of the National Education Association during the 1880's, while probably faithfully representing the sentiments of a majority of the educational profession, should not be considered as reflecting substantial unanimity of the profession at any time during the ten-year period. In the professional and public press, in conventions, on lecture platforms, and before Congressional committees, educators vigorously debated the essentiality, the propriety, the constitutionality, and the wisdom of enacting federal aid legislation. It is clear that, among those educators who publicized their views, a large majority favored passage of the Blair bill throughout the decade, but a sizable, influential, and constantly growing minority as consistently advocated the bill's defeat.

The case for enactment can be reconstructed from the statements of city and state school superintendents, the agents of the Peabody and Slater funds, Commissioner Eaton, and others prominent in the field of public education. A few representatives of higher education, both public and private, joined in the

[34]*Congressional Record*, 48:1, 2008.

advocacy of the Blair bill; most college and university officials and private school leaders were to be found among the opposition. The proponents within the profession maintained that:

1. Universal, equalized education was essential to the perpetuation of "free institutions" and the Federal Government was obligated to insure to all children at least an elementary education.[35]

2. "Of the constitutionality of Federal aid there is hardly a peg to hang a doubt upon." The assistance hitherto provided by the national government to educational endeavors and other internal improvements had established unshakable precedent for the enactment of the Blair bill.[36]

3. Despite magnificent efforts of the South to improve its educational status, national aid was nevertheless essential. "It is impossible in her impoverished condition for her to furnish the means of education to the masses of the children."[37]

4. The prolonged withholding of federal assistance from the Southern educational systems had produced a certain despair among Southern citizenry, causing a decline in the extent of local public support of education; "there has been a relative loss in our educational status."[38]

5. The Federal Government, having freed and enfranchised the Negroes, was obligated to "fit them for the temptations and responsibilities of citizenship. . . . Negroes are the wards of the nation." This was a burden the Southern states were not prepared to shoulder alone, nor were they desirous of doing so.[39]

6. This was not purely sectional legislation, and, while the

[35]Connecticut State Board of Education, resolution, *Congressional Record*, 48:1, 2007.

[36]W. W. W. Jones, Superintendent of Public Instruction of Nebraska, *The Critic*, May, 1886, 267. This monthly conducted a poll of the attitudes of educators toward the Blair bill, the responses to which were published during April and May, 1886.

[37]J. L. M. Curry, "Federal Aid to Education," *U. S. Bureau of Education Circular No. 3, 1884*, 93; and Hugh Thompson, Superintendent of Public Instruction of South Carolina, before House of Representatives Committee on Education and Labor, *Congressional Record*, 48:1, 2004.

[38]William P. Johnston, president of Tulane University, in a letter to Senator Blair, quoted by him in *Congressional Record*, 50:1, 275.

[39]Curry, *op. cit.*, and James S. Hook, School Commissioner of Georgia, in *Report of the Commissioner of Education for the Year 1887-1888*, 167.

preponderance of its benefits would be felt in the South, the entire nation would benefit from its application.[40]

7. Without the participation of the national government in the support of public education, too great a proportion of the control of educational opportunity would reside in the churches or other non-public agencies. This would "limit that great work to a few, or to the ruling classes, or to those who could pay, an idea consistent only with the great illiteracy and degradation of the masses."[41]

8. In addition to the crying need for federal aid, the economic condition of the country demanded such legislation immediately —"When the surplus in the Treasury has so contracted the circulating currency as to threaten the destruction of the commerce of the country and to seriously damage every business enterprise." No more legitimate or economically sound method for returning this money to circulation than aid to education could be devised.[42]

9. The granting of federal aid to states deficient in educational facilities would stimulate local efforts, "by revealing the advantages of better schools." Only then would such areas be encouraged to maintain these institutions for themselves.[43]

10. Federal aid was essential because "public education on a more liberal basis is the only solution to the "capital and labor" question now so seriously threatening our country, and the only means by which the spirit of communism and anarchism is to be driven from our land."[44]

In similar fashion, the position of those educational leaders who opposed federal aid and the Blair bill can be reviewed. Here, too, were to be found many city and state school super-

[40]J. H. Smart, Superintendent of Public Instruction of Indiana, before House of Representatives Committee on Education and Labor, *Congressional Record*, 48:1, 2005.

[41]John Eaton, "The Nation, The Only Patron of Education Equal to the Present Emergency," *Education*, 26:336, March, 1884.

[42]Solomon Palmer, Superintendent of Education of Alabama, quoted in Commissioner of Education Report, *op. cit.*, *1887-1888*, 167-168.

[43]George A. Littlefield, Superintendent of Schools of Newport, R. I., *The Critic, op. cit.*, 268.

[44]J. A. B. Lovett, "Federal Aid," *U. S. Bureau of Education Circular of Information, No. 6, 1888*, 146.

intendents, and these were apparently joined by a majority of the public and private college and university administrators. The arguments of those members of the profession who disapproved of this legislation held that:

1. Not only was federal aid in the form proposed by the Blair bill unconstitutional; it was also the first step in the direction of complete national control of education. "We no more want a department of the General Government controlling education throughout the nation than we want a department of public worship."[45]

2. In the South, there had occurred a great awakening to the need for support of education which had demonstrated that the South was able to provide for itself. Moneys from the federal treasury would serve to destroy a growing sense of self-reliance and would "impede the progress of popular education in the South."[46]

3. The claim that the presence of millions of illiterate enfranchised Negroes constituted an emergency was a "subterfuge." The Negro "is dependent, kind-hearted and trustful, and certainly is not the character to plot rebellion, anarchy, communism, etc. If let alone, he will work out his own salvation in this country."[47]

4. It was indefensible to legislate federal grants of money to states which did not need them, "in order to have a pretext . . . for squandering other and larger millions upon States which we assume (mistakenly) to have need of them." Northern states, for whom the need of aid did not exist, were thus to be placated with a "largess or bribe" to obtain their support for payments to Southern states where the need was also non-existent.[48]

[45]E. P. Seaver, Superintendent of Schools of Boston, Massachusetts, *Congressional Record*, 50:1, 9; Oscar H. Cooper, Superintendent of Public Instruction of Texas, *ibid.*

[46]S. C. Armstrong, Principal of Hampton Normal and Agricultural Institute, quoted in Lynchburg *Virginian*, January 9, 1888; A. P. Marble, Superintendent of Schools of Worcester, Mass., letter to New York *Evening Post*, January 9, 1888.

[47]J. M. Greenwood, Superintendent of Schools, Kansas City, Mo., *Critic, op. cit.*, 267.

[48]F. A. P. Barnard, President of Columbia College, letter to *Critic, op. cit.*, 265.

5. The introduction of federal assistance into local public educational situations would result in the waste of vast sums of money—it was likely that much of such grants would never reach the local schools but would be "frittered away"—and "politics" and patronage would invade the common school.[49]

6. The Blair bill would operate to reward "the lack of endeavor, of which illiteracy is the expression." It would place "a premium on illiteracy and local neglect of education," and was comparable to a system of awarding bounties for "idle and truant boys." Federal aid, if given at all, should be granted on the basis of the reduction of illiteracy in a state—i.e. the greater the local effort, the more federal assistance should be provided.[50]

7. The Blair bill, while requiring states to match the federal grants, was predicated upon the assumption that certain states were too poor to support education independently. If they were able to match an annually increasing appropriation, they were ipso facto able to increase their own local efforts, hence federal assistance was not necessary.[51]

8. Great popular support for this legislation did not exist. "It is a mistake to assume that the teachers of the South universally desire the passage of the Blair bill." Many state educational organizations opposed or ignored it, and certain national associations which proclaimed unanimous support for federal aid were able to muster resolutions favoring the Blair bill only after debate had been stifled and most convention members had left the meetings. Even "public opinion . . . is now drifting steadily and rapidly" in the direction of complete disavowal of the entire federal aid principle.[52]

The Critic, a literary review having a circulation of approximately 5,000 during the 1880's,[53] found the Blair bill a suf-

---

[49]Marble, *op. cit.*

[50]William T. Welcher, Superintendent of Schools of California, *The Critic, op. cit.*, 266; Thomas C. Chamberlain, President of University of Wisconsin, *Congressional Record*, 50:1, 9.

[51]A. P. Marble, "The Blair Bill," *U. S. Bureau of Education Circular of Information No. 6, 1888*, 150.

[52]Barnard, *op. cit.*; Cooper, *op. cit.*; Marble, New York *Evening Post, op. cit.*

[53]Frank Luther Mott, *The History of American Magazines*, III, 551.

ficiently important issue in 1886 to conduct a rather careful investigation of the sentiments of professional educators regarding federal aid. Though apparently without any particular political allegiance, *The Critic* was editorially opposed to this legislation, but it opened its columns to favorable as well as unfavorable comment. During April and May, 1886, *The Critic* published letters received from state and city superintendents of schools and university presidents in answer to the magazine's request for a statement regarding the Blair bill.[54] From this canvass, as well as on the basis of the numerous statements of individual educators, a fairly representative picture of the opinions of educational administrators throughout the nation is obtainable.

It is noteworthy that the greatest professional opposition to the Blair bill centered in New England—where the public schools were deemed adequate and the supporters of private education exerted a disproportionate degree of political influence—and in Texas, where, unlike all other Southern states, fabulous state land revenues were beginning to be made available to educational enterprise, causing the educators and representatives of that state to reject suggestions of federal aid. Few college or university presidents were to be found championing the cause of federal support for education. Eliot of Harvard, F. A. P. Barnard of Columbia College, James B. Angell of the University of Michigan, and others bitterly denounced such proposals. It was evident that within the profession the leadership of the proponents of federal aid had been taken over by state and city superintendents from the Middle West, while Southern professional support remained strong.

What might be termed the educational press also entered into the debate over federal assistance. Despite the widespread opposition to the Blair bills in New England, one of the most spirited campaigns in its behalf carried on by any pedagogical periodical was that of the *Journal of Education* of Boston. This journal was the product of a merger in 1875 of "all the important periodicals devoted to education" in New England,[55] and

---

[54]See footnote 36, p. 111, *et seq.*
[55]Mott, *op. cit.*, 168.

its prestige and influence by the middle 1880's were considerable. Under its editor, T. W. Bicknell, the *Journal* supported the Blair bill consistently throughout the decade. In 1882, it decried the "constitutional holdbacks" in Congress who blocked every attempt to further public education, but noted its belief that the national controls proposed by the Hoar bill would never be accepted by the American people.[56] The *Journal's* position was aptly summarized in 1883 when one of its contributors commented that:

It is folly for a people to organize themselves into a free State, and attempt to promote or to perpetuate its institutions, without providing by law for universal education, which shall be at the same time compulsory and free. . . . It is in accordance with a sound philosophy for the National Government to do anything and everything, as far as its ability extends, which is necessary to be done for its own preservation and for the development of its people, and which the States or the people cannot do as individuals acting alone.[57]

In another publication under Bicknell's direction, the magazine *Education* ("an international technical and philosophical journal"), there was indicated an even more vigorous advocacy of the position of the Federal Government in relation to local education. In an article disapproving of any distribution of federal funds without adequate federal supervision, it was maintained that the money

should be paid directly to districts by educated and responsible agents appointed by the executive, and on such conditions as to improve and lengthen schools already existing, and to secure the establishment of others in localities where they are needed. These school agents should act in harmony with local officials . . . but be independent of State control, and required to . . . report in detail to the Commissioner of Education.[58]

The *School Journal*, an established educational weekly published in New York City and Chicago and edited by Amos Kellogg and Francis W. Parker, attempted to straddle the federal

---

[56]*Journal of Education*, Boston, 15:24-25, January 12, 1882.

[57]J. W. Dickinson, "National Aid for Public Schools," *Journal of Education*, Boston, 18:227-228, October 11, 1883.

[58]J. W. Patterson, "National Aid to Education," *Education*, 1:418-419, May, 1881.

aid question. Early in 1886, an editorial favoring federal assistance appeared in which it was demanded that federal support
should produce "Schools where REAL geography, REAL history, REAL arithmetic, and REAL science will be taught,"
and in which "downright, upright, honest, outspoken religion"
would be included in the curriculum.[59] But one month later,
the *School Journal* in commenting upon the Senate's passage of
the Blair bill complained that "We have enough of political influence in education already. It is our daily prayer that the bles-
sed time may speedily come when politicians will let education
alone. It has never hurt them, and we can't imagine what grudge
they have that they should want to hurt it."[60]

The most outspoken criticism of federal aid to appear in any
educational journal was published by the magazine *Academy*,
a New York State "Journal of Secondary Education" which
served as the organ of the Associated Academic Principals of
that state. The *Academy*, which apparently catered to public
high school and private school administrators, followed the line
laid down by the leaders in higher education. Its concern was
not primarily for the constitutionality of a federal assistance
program but rather for what it conceived to be the deleterious
effects of such measures upon the states. "While therefore under
the Blair bill more Southern voters would be able to read ten
years hence, the states would have purchased their education at
the cost of those essential qualities which go to make the states
of the North what they are." In company with many others,
the *Academy* considered that the South was progressing satisfactorily without governmental assistance and that aid would
only result in a relaxation of local efforts.[61]

As will be made evident, the consideration of this issue by
professional publications was insignificant in comparison with
its treatment by the general lay press. Many pedagogical journals ignored the matter altogether, and others gave it only the
most cursory attention. In clarity of argument, depth of under-

[59]*School Journal*, February 20, 1886, 116.
[60]*Ibid.*, March 20, 1886, 180.
[61]"National Aid to Southern Education," *Academy*, 1:65, March, 1886.

standing of the educational and political issues involved, and thorough analysis of the pros and cons, the professional press was relatively deficient. One has only to cite the efforts of *The Critic* referred to earlier and the remarkably vigorous campaign of the New York *Evening Post*, yet to be described, to indicate the rather glaring weakness of the educational publications. Perhaps professional opinion would have been more effectively mobilized had there existed a more dynamic professional press.

The Churches

The interest of a substantial number of religious leaders in the federal aid issue during the 1880's has been indicated by mention of the National Education Assembly, a temporary organization formed specifically to deal with this question and acting largely under the leadership and sponsorship of various Protestant denominations. That the religious community was not unanimous in support of the Blair bill follows automatically from the previously established position of the Catholic Church in opposition to any form of federal assistance. The Blair bill, however, produced more concern—and more opposition—from non-Catholic churches than had any of the earlier proposals to legislate federal support for education.

The resolution and petition adopted by the National Education Assembly, favoring aid that "will stimulate rather than supersede" local efforts and that will be "immediate and not remote," was signed by leaders of the Congregational, Methodist, Baptist, and Presbyterian churches. There is no indication that other denominations participated in the Assembly, but Senator Blair, in presenting this memorial to the Senate, reported that "there is a substantial combination of all the great religious bodies of the country, at least in the Northern states, who have one specific purpose, and that is to urge upon Congress the appropriation of national money in the direction of general education."[62] That Blair's reference to "all" denominations did not include the Catholic Church was doubtless self-evident, but

[62]*Congressional Record*, 48:1, 2003.

there were indications that, in addition to the denominations whose members had signed the petition, the Episcopalian leadership was also in sympathy with the Blair measure. *The Churchman*, a prominent organ of that sect, went on record in favor of the bill during the debates of 1886 and 1888. While its approval can only be termed moderate, *The Churchman* indicated considerable concern over the problem of illiteracy in the South. It did suggest a modification to the Blair scheme when it indicated that perhaps all federal funds should be used to promote industrial schools as the surest means of fostering moral training and developing self-reliance.[63]

A far stronger advocate of federal aid was the *Andover Review*, a Congregational monthly whose "important career" included a notable series of editorials regarding the common schools in the mid-1880's.[64] This series contained an article by Edmund J. James, leading professor of economics at the University of Pennsylvania and founder of the American Academy of Political and Social Science, which went beyond the provisions of the Blair bill in advocating federal participation in local educational affairs. Noting that popular elections and the increasing mobility of the population forced national interest in education, the writer held no qualms regarding the constitutionality of federal assistance. He proposed that the national government should deal "directly with the people of the United States" and should administer its grants through its own agencies or through local offices federally approved. Curiously, however, this advocate added that "The Federal government should not interfere with the local administration of schools."[65] There were few who felt, as he apparently did, that federal administration of the grants-in-aid could permit totally independent local operation.

Disagreement as to the desirability of federal aid was characteristic of many of the Protestant sects, however. Another,

---

[63]*The Churchman*, 53:228-229, February 27, 1886, and 57:248-249, March 3, 1888.

[64]Mott, *op. cit.*, 76, 164.

[65]E. J. James, "National Aid to Popular Education," *Andover Review*, 5:250-262, March, 1886.

and apparently more influential Congregational periodical gave voice to decided antipathy toward federal support in any form. This was the *New Englander*, a magazine whose purpose was to "give utterance to the New England way of thinking," which, says Mott, meant a spirit of Congregationalism, whiggery, promotion of education, and moral orthodoxy. Though decidedly anti-Catholic, the *New Englander* found itself in Catholic company in its opposition to the Blair bill. It maintained until its demise in 1885 "a respectable and influential position. . . . It was one of the best of the religious quarterlies."[66] In the midst of the Blair bill debate in 1886, one of its contributors, voicing extreme concern for the depressed status of Southern Negroes, opined that "no legislative remedy has yet been proposed" to deal with the problem of improving that condition. It was here maintained that the advancement of education in the South since the war had been "remarkable and satisfactory" and that the only way to produce a permanently improved educational situation was through the application of continued local effort and private benefactions. Nationally imposed and perforce politically polluted federal subsidies, in this writer's view, were not the remedy; furthermore, he considered such legislation unconstitutional.[67]

One of the most active of all journals fighting the Blair bill was the *New Princeton Review*, which, though by the 1880's officially disconnected from denominational control, possessed a strong Presbyterian heritage. In a series of unsigned editorials (written perhaps by the editor, William H. Sloane) its position was never in doubt. Objection to the Blair bill was based on political and "religious" grounds. The *Review* maintained that the "question of relation and proportion between central and local powers" in a federal system was paramount in the analysis of "our most imminent problems, especially those of political economy and education." The Blair bill it considered a "monstrous proposal" in that it was "a scheme for the creation of a new

[66]Mott, *op. cit.*, II, 312-315.
[67]Daniel H. Chamberlain, "Present Aspects of the Southern Question," *New Englander and Yale Review*, 9:26-33, January, 1886.

Federal bureau and an interference with the rights and duties of individual states" which would lead "ultimately to the centralization of the entire public school system." The *Review* did, however, recognize and admit the great need for some sort of concerted effort to eliminate illiteracy and proposed a federal aid bill to meet what it called an "unprecedented national emergency." This proposal involved temporary grants to be made only where needed and administration exclusively in the hands of state officials. Compulsory education was also deemed essential.

Objection to the Blair measure on "religious" grounds was even more definite.

It is impossible to doubt that such a system of national education administered by the Federal Government would be peremptorily dissociated from all positive religious teaching. [All sects and denominations] would each protest against the teachings of opinions contrary to their own. . . . [and] absolute silence on religious questions [would result]. . . . In view of these facts, we are thoroughly convinced that such a comprehensive and centralized scheme of national education, if once thoroughly realized would prove the most appalling enginery for the propagation of anti-Christian and atheistic unbelief, and of anti-social nihilistic ethics, individual, social, and political, which this sin-rent world has ever seen.[68]

It was Catholic influence, however, which Senator Blair credited with being the strongest sectarian enemy of his legislative proposals. In his peroration to the debate of 1888, Blair labeled the New York *Evening Post* and the Washington *Post*, leading journalistic opponents of federal aid, as "organs of Jesuitism." There was, said Blair, "a great fight initiating and already outlining itself for the future between the common schools of the United States and those influences which would subvert this great system. . . . Upon the staff of every great paper of this country to-day is a Jesuit, and the business of that man is to see that a blow is struck whenever there is an opportunity to strike at the common school system of America. . . ."[69]

[68]"The Political Situation," *New Princeton Review*, 1:62-77; and "Education Bills Before Congress," *ibid.*, 2:131-134, July, 1886. See also *Ibid.*, "Federal Aid to Education," 1:210-216, March, 1886.

[69]*Congressional Record*, 50:1, 1218.

This accusation was, of course, stoutly denied by Catholic spokesmen, and, in the case of the New York *Evening Post*, which led the assault on the bill, it was altogether groundless. Nevertheless, despite claims that "Catholics had nothing to do with" the campaign against federal aid, the Church's publications carried on the opposition to such a program which had been inaugurated at the time of the Hoar bill debate. One of the leading clerical journals, *The American Catholic Quarterly Review*, which enjoyed the support and sponsorship of many Catholic leaders and whose policy included a lively interest in education,[70] undertook in 1888 to summarize in some detail the position of the Church regarding the Blair bill. All the usual arguments in opposition were reviewed: the measure's unconstitutionality, the belief that such legislation was a phase of a plot to centralize all public education and subordinate local to federal educational officials, the indefensibility of an apportionment system based on total rather than school-age illiteracy, and the increasing efforts in the South to improve educational facilities which made federal assistance unnecessary. The *Quarterly* went further, however, and pronounced the federal aid plan a scheme to destroy the Catholic Church and its educational system in the United States. It ridiculed the concern of many who were demanding that no federal funds be used to support sectarian schools by contending that the public schools of the North were already "sectarian" since, the *Quarterly* claimed, ninety-nine out of every hundred teachers were Protestants and the textbooks were similarly inclined. Blair was labeled the "mouthpiece" of those who, crying that only non-sectarian education should be supported, were actually desirous of subsidizing schools under Protestant control, and he was credited with "a hatred of Catholicity [which] had evidently been a concealed but powerful motor in all his acts, some now verging on madness."

The bill itself was pronounced the absurd scheme of a social dreamer, desirous of making his "pet theories . . . the groundwork for voting away millions of money wrung from the

[70]Mott, *op. cit.*, III, 69.

people." Such legislation, maintained the *Quarterly*, was opposed by many Senators, who found it politically inexpedient to vote against any measure intended to promote education, but who trusted that the Supreme Court would declare the measure unconstitutional. In words almost identical to those arising out of Presbyterian disapproval as expressed in the *New Princeton Review* articles, the *American Catholic Quarterly Review* found the core of its objections to lie on similarly religious grounds.

Education when based on religion and morality is a good; without such control it may be and must be a curse and not a blessing to any community. . . . now all reference to God and prayer and eternity is carefully expunged from books adopted in the common schools of this country. . . . If the control of all the public schools in the country is allowed to be grasped by the Federal Government, the rationalizing process becomes comparatively easy. Instead of laboring to effect the dechristianizing scheme in State after State, the whole effort can be concentrated at Washington.[71]

It is worthy of note that, challenged by the Blair bill and its apparent popularity, many Protestant leaders found themselves joining the Catholics to oppose such legislation. It is evident that there was considerable agreement as to the bases for opposition—both groups feared centralization of educational control as an atheistic, non-Christian tendency and held that federal support, which to them was tantamount to control, meant an even greater reduction in the common-school's concern for religion, morality, and ethics. The Catholic hierarchy, however, nursed an even greater fear—that any form of federal participation in public school education would be followed by national legislation abolishing denominational schools. The influence of such denominational statements as these is difficult to assess, although the senatorial proponents of federal aid made much of the pronouncements of sectarian leaders who were favorable to the bill. Suffice it to say here that, except for the Catholic Church, lack of unanimity on the question of federal aid legislation characterized the religious groups to an extent fully comparable to the disunity existing within the educational profession itself.

[71] J. G. Shea, "Federal Schemes to Aid Common Schools in the Southern States," *American Catholic Quarterly Review*, 13:345-359, April, 1888.

The Press

In contrast to the previous decade, the 1880's was featured by newspaper coverage of the national educational problem which far outweighed the attention it received from periodicals. As the acuteness of educational deficiencies became more evident, and as a result of the almost continuous consideration of the Blair bill, newspapers from all sections of the country awoke to the significance of the problem of school support. It is not an overstatement to say that one of the decisive factors in producing the bill's defeat was the opposition campaign conducted by one New York newspaper. Magazines, too, awarded more space to discussions of this issue than had heretofore been the case, but this increased attention was in no way comparable to the surge of newspaper interest.

MAGAZINES

Among national magazines, *Harper's Monthly* continued to stand as the most outspoken supporter of federal aid to the common schools. Contributors to the monthly reasserted their devotion to free public education and, as each new proposal of federal assistance appeared, maintained the position that the urgency and the constitutionality of national support could not be denied. Congress must be generous "for the education of those ... who now can not read the ballots which they cast." Legislation on the order of the Blair bill—and *Harper's* editors expressed the desire that national aid should be even more munificent than there provided—represented both the "right" and the "duty" of the Federal Government. It must be noted, however, that after 1885, the traditional interest heretofore shown by *Harper's* in the federal aid question disappeared, paralleling a decline in interest evidenced in the Congress and, to a considerable extent, over the nation as a whole.[72]

Of all magazines with a sizable national circulation, *The Century Illustrated Monthly* magazine provided the closest approach to an open forum on the federal aid question during the

[72]C. F. Thwing, "The National Government and Education," *Harper's New Monthly Magazine*, 68:471-476, February, 1884.

1880's. The *Century*, which was the continuation of *Scribner's Monthly* under a management independent of the Scribner's book publishing interests, continued its predecessor's noncommittal policy regarding national school support. Contributors on both sides were welcomed, but the magazine itself apparently took no stand. Its issues of 1884 were featured by a debate between a Northerner and a North Carolinian on the question of the constitutionality and the desirability of federal assistance to the local schools, in which the traditional positions were reversed. While the North Carolinian argued for the Blair bill, presenting the usual defenses of its propriety and essentiality, the Northern opponent maintained that unless such legislation could be established as constitutional, "the question of its expediency and adaptability to its purpose is of little importance." A somewhat novel opposition argument was presented when this writer submitted that, inasmuch as the Constitution granted control of the suffrage to the individual states, "the nation has no right to complain if the voters furnished by the States are not to its liking." It was here contended that only an amendment to the Constitution, which specifically empowered the national government to participate in local educational activities, could effectively and legally cope with the problem. Another contributor entered a plea for more extensive press coverage of the educational problem and of the needs of the South generally. Sensing the widespread public unfamiliarity with the Southern situation, this writer commended the major newspapers and magazines for their concern with this issue, but noted that "the network of local publications, through which the masses are best reached, have barely touched upon the subject." As with *Harper's*, however, *Century* did not maintain an active interest in the federal aid question throughout the decade. After 1885, discussion of the matter rarely appeared in its pages.[73]

[73]J. B. Peterson, "National Aid to Education," *Century Magazine*, 28:790-792, March, 1884.

J. Allen Holt, "National Aid to Education—A Reply," *Century Magazine*, 28:156-157, May, 1884.

C. N. Jenkins, "A Plea for National Aid to Education," *Century*, 30:810-811, September, 1885.

Certain other magazines of some national account, while actively and continuously interested in general educational topics, rather completely ignored the federal aid issue. A few articles appear to have stood as mild rebuttals to those who were maintaining that public education was non-Christian education,[74] or as reaffirmations of the desirability that, in education, Church and State remain separate. It is not unlikely that, as the ultimate fate of the Blair bill became more certain, many editors concluded that discussion of the question had become academic.

Opposition to the Blair bill was the active concern of at least three magazines which could boast of a position of some national prominence. One of these was *The Critic*, the non-partisan literary review whose poll of educational leaders on the Blair bill has already been mentioned. Although opening its pages to both supporters and antagonists of the federal aid proposals, *The Critic* itself was decidedly opposed to such legislation. Not only did it consider the bill unconstitutional and potentially harmful to Southern local self-reliance, it further accused the bill's proponents, and in particular its author, of demagogism. Commenting on a letter which Blair had written to the Boston *Globe* in 1886, in which he had stressed the idea that his measure constituted a means of distributing "accumulated property to the children of the common schools, and is therefore . . . a relief from the alarming inequalities which now prevail in the possession of wealth," *The Critic* retorted that "It is no part of the American scheme of government to equalize the distribution of wealth, by free-will offerings to the poor. . . ."[75] Like many other opponents of the Blair bill, *The Critic* considered the measure to be one of relief and not of reconstruction.

A somewhat more influential opposition periodical, to judge by its circulation—which grew from 7,500 in 1880 to 17,000 in 1889—was the *North American Review*. Under the editorship during this period of Allen Thorndike Rice, this journal emphasized history and politics, attempted to maintain a certain politi-

---

[74]Horace E. Scudder, "The Church, The State, and the School," *Atlantic Monthly*, 63:786-793, June, 1889.
[75]*The Critic*, 8:265, May, 1886.

cal neutrality, and evidenced considerable concern for what it believed to be abuses in the operation of the common schools.[76] With regard to federal aid, however, the selection of articles for publication indicated a rather pronounced bias against the Blair bill or, indeed, any federal participation in local education. An article authored by Senator Ingalls of Kansas, a leading Republican opponent of the measure, described the Blair bill as badly devised for the purpose it was presumed to serve and vigorously denied the urgency of that purpose—the need of the South for help. The South, wrote the Senator, was economically and financially as able as other sections to support education unassisted—"What they require is vigorous preaching of the gospel of work"—and the implication that any state outside the South needed aid was "degrading." While articles specifically directed toward the Blair bill were sparse in the *North American Review*, a significant series of essays on the function of the State by the English author, Ouida, was given considerable prominence. In these writings, all tendencies, of whatever nature, toward governmental centralization of the assumption of local prerogatives by the State were bitterly castigated. In effect, regulatory controls over any aspect of social activity were vehemently denounced, and this included all national concern for the conduct of education in any country.[77] Articles of this kind, unaccompanied by contributed or editorial expressions of the opposite viewpoint, suggest the presence of an attitude decidedly unsympathetic to federal aid legislation.

It was not until the introduction of the Blair bill that the *Nation* took an active part in the discussion of this type of federal legislation, despite the fact that its listed purposes included the improvement of conditions in the South and among the Negroes and the fixing of "public attention on the importance of public education." But throughout the 1880's, the *Nation* stood in the forefront of journalistic opposition to federal aid and this

[76]Mott, *op. cit.*, II, 220-254, III, 163.

[77]John James Ingalls, "National Aid to Common Schools," *North American Review*, 142:381-386, April, 1886.

Ouida, "The State as an Immoral Teacher," *North American Review*, 153:193-204, August, 1891.

position cannot have been other than potent in the extreme. James Russell Lowell said of the *Nation* that its "discussions of politics had done more good and influenced public opinion more than any other agency, or all others combined, in the country." This was, of course, a tribute to its editors, Edward L. Godkin, who in 1881 left the *Nation* to edit the New York *Evening Post* from where the anti-federal aid campaign was carried on even more strenuously, and Wendell Phillips Garrison. Mott sets the maximum circulation of the *Nation* during the 1880's at 12,000 but implies that no other periodical was so thoroughly or generally read by the leading figures of the period. Godkin's assumption of the *Post* editorship, which, in Mott's phrase, made of the *Nation* "the weekly edition of the Post," meant that *Nation* comments represented the views of both Godkin and Garrison.[78]

Throughout the decade, the *Nation* reported upon the status of the Blair bill and editorialized in opposition. Typical of these comments is the following which appeared in April, 1884, after the bill's first passage of the Senate.

There seems to be no reason for the bill except the fact that there is in some States much illiteracy with which the local authorities do not try to cope effectually, and that there is in the United States Treasury a good deal of surplus money. That the distribution will cease at the end of ten years, we have no expectation. . . . the local sense of responsibility for popular education, and willingness to make sacrifices for it, will be steadily weakened in the very States in which it is most necessary they should be strong, from the first day on which the jingle of Federal school money is heard. The experiment is, therefore, a momentous one. Its educational features are probably far less important than the political ones.[79]

It was in the New York *Evening Post*, however, that this group of opposition leaders made its liveliest and most effective campaign. Much of what appeared in the *Nation* on this subject was mere review or repetition of the attack launched by that newspaper.

Perhaps the exhaustiveness of the Congressional debates on the

[78]Mott, *op. cit.*, III, 333-344.
[79]*The Nation*, April, 1884, 305.

Blair bill and the intensity of feeling reflected in certain newspapers led magazine editors to neglect the federal aid issue as one which needed no further attention. It seems evident, in view of the dimensions of the problem, the implications of the proposed legislation, and the not inconsequential public interest which had developed, that magazines generally failed to perform adequately. It is doubtful that they played any significant role either in shaping opinion or in analyzing the issues presented by Congressional consideration of the question of federal participation in education.

NEWSPAPERS

Not so the newspapers. The Blair bill, together with some of its immediate predecessors, occasioned more journalistic comment and analysis than had any previous national educational issue. All sections of the country participated, though to decidedly varying degrees. As was to be expected, the sections which would have been most acutely affected by the measure were those whose newspapers were, on the whole, most active. This was not entirely true, however, since, for reasons of editorial preeminence, the New York City newspapers were the most energetic participants in the journalistic debate. It is interesting to note that, in general, Southern newspapers were allied with those of Boston in support of the Blair bill, while Far-Western dailies and most of the New York City journals were joined in opposition.

The Far West. In the Far West, the traditional disinterest in federal aid legislation which had characterized those most distant and relatively favored states continued to dominate editorial expression. The San Francisco, California, *Evening Bulletin,* a "radical, crusading . . . clean, family" paper,[80] afforded the question only cursory reportorial mention until the introduction of the Blair bill in 1884. On that occasion, the *Bulletin* was moved to complain about the large number of bills proposing to dole out federal moneys for various purposes which it considered purely

[80]Frank Luther Mott, *American Journalism: A History of Newspapers in the United States Through 250 Years 1690 to 1940,* 474.

political. Specifically with regard to the Blair bill, it commented that "the Republicans are prepared to . . . suggest a large appropriation by the National Government, apparently for general school purposes, but really to secure the wavering political allegiance of the colored men of the South." Following the bill's passage of the Senate in 1888, the *Bulletin* reaffirmed its dislike of such legislation, labeling the measure unsound "on financial, educational, moral, [and] perhaps constitutional grounds." The newspaper felt that the South no longer needed the projected aid and that Southerners rightfully considered the bill an "insult."[81]

A similar attitude was apparently characteristic of the Salt Lake City, Utah, *Daily Tribune*, an anti-Mormon newspaper which held the largest circulation in the Rocky Mountain area during the 1880's.[82] On the issue of federal control of education, the *Tribune* maintained: "The principle that where the National money goes, there goes also the National authority and supervision is a correct one . . . indeed, we do not see how it can be safely ignored." Fearing the relaxation of local efforts if such a bill were to become law, and disapproving of the basis for appropriation contained in the Blair bill, the *Tribune* hoped for revisions in the measure, but concluded that "if the change should kill it altogether, there would be no occasion for wet eyes."[83] Subsequent attention to the progress of this legislation was meager, reflecting the general public disinterest which pervaded the region.

New England. While the Far-Western and Middle-Western dailies (i.e. Chicago *Tribune*, Milwaukee *Sentinel*, and St. Paul *Pioneer-Press*) generally evidenced disinterest in or expressed mild disapproval of the Blair bill, the newspapers of the Eastern seaboard and the Old South vigorously joined the battle. Boston newspapers were preponderantly in favor of the proposal, at least until 1888. The Boston *Herald*, with a circulation which by 1890 had reached 140,000, placing it among the most widely

[81]San Francisco *Evening Bulletin*, March 24, 1884, February 16, 1888.
[82]Mott, *op. cit.*, 477.
[83]Salt Lake City *Daily Tribune*, April 9, 1884.

circulated half-dozen journals of the country, called for the enactment of the bill. Although a generally "conservative" paper,[84] the *Herald* questioned the opposition charges that the South was unfit to use wisely the proposed aid. "If . . . the Southern States are unable to give instruction to their children and youth, and will not be able to do so, for ten or twenty years to come, and are willing to receive and properly apply national aid, without relaxing any effort of their own, we think the nation is in duty bound to assist them, and should do so in self-defense against the menace of an ignorant suffrage."[85] Similar sentiments were voiced by the Boston *Traveller*, which called the opponents of the bill "short-sighted, even when basing their opposition on economical grounds. True economy demands the building of the school house and the establishment of the school, since on these the safety and perpetuity of our institutions depend."[86] The Boston *Journal* expressed indignation at those who were accusing the Southern states of embarking upon a program to encourage the increase of ignorance in order thereby to profit further from federal grants should the Blair bill become law. "We have not so poor an opinion of any State in this Union as to believe that its people would deliberately cultivate illiteracy and diminish educational influences in order that a few thousand dollars more might be drawn from the national Treasury." The *Journal* observed that illiteracy was a "disease" and declared its conviction that "If there is any better or more natural course than to apportion the remedy in ratio to the extent of the disease, we do not know what it is. . . . the security of all our institutions depends ultimately upon an intelligent ballot."[87]

The South. Southern newspapers were preponderantly, but not exclusively, supporters of the Blair bill and the federal assistance principle. Many journals, although staunchly Democratic in their politics, broke with the official party line as set forth in the platforms—as did many southern Democratic Sen-

[84]Mott, *op. cit.*, 403, 452, 560.
[85]Boston *Herald*, February 9, 1886.
[86]Boston *Traveller*, February 18, 1886.
[87]Boston *Journal*, February 18, 1886.

ators—and these were joined by the organs of certain renegade groups, such as the Richmond, Virginia, *Whig*, which acted largely in the interests of the Virginia Readjuster party. In contrast to the journalistic attention afforded this measure in other sections, that given by the Southern newspapers was both more consistent and of longer duration, although here too a decrease in newspaper concern is perceptible after 1886. However, as was to be expected, the newspapers of no other section evidenced as much interest as did those of the South, and, outside New York City, the efforts of such dailies as the Richmond *Whig* and the Louisville, Kentucky, *Courier-Journal* were not surpassed.

Southern newspaper editors continually published pleas to the Representatives and Senators of the South to act with dispatch in enacting federal aid legislation. Senators who opposed the Blair bill on grounds of unconstitutionality were bitterly castigated by the New Orleans *Daily Picayune* and the Charleston, South Carolina, *News and Courier*.[88] The New Orleans *Times-Democrat* accused such legislators of finding "the Constitution opposed to the best interests of the people" and indirectly attacked certain of the region's political practices by hinting that the Blair bill "can not be refused unless we believe that there is some virtue in illiteracy."[89] One of the most vicious attacks upon the constitutional basis for opposition appeared in the Birmingham, Alabama, *Age* during the debate of 1886, specifically directed against one of the Alabama Senators who was then engaged in leading the fight against the Blair bill.

The distinguished Senator does not antagonize the bill this time altogether on the ground of its unconstitutionality, but he lays down the broad principle that the Government has no right to tax one man to educate the children of another man; not only this, but the Senator intimated that the best people in the United States were uneducated backwoodsmen. . . . we are bound to infer . . . that the Senator doubts the wisdom of educating the masses of the people. . . . Sen-

[88]New Orleans *Daily Picayune*, February 13, 1886; Charleston, S. C., *News and Courier*, 1889, selections reproduced in *Congressional Record*, 50:1, 747.
[89]New Orleans *Times-Democrat*, quoted in *Congressional Record*, 49:1, 1731.

ator Morgan is perfectly sincere in his views on public education, but he is a century and a half behind the age in which he lives.[90]

In a statement which indicates, though rather naively, the intensity of feeling regarding the political importance of the Blair bill, the Portsmouth, Virginia, *Enterprise,* on the occasion of the measure's third introduction in 1887, maintained that: "Should the Democrats in the House of Representatives fail to pass it, there will not be the remotest chance of Virginia and North Carolina casting their electoral votes for the Democratic candidates for the presidency next fall . . . we believe we know the sentiment of the people of Virginia, especially upon this measure."[91]

One of the most consistent champions in the South for the Blair bill was the Richmond *Whig.* Decidedly unsympathetic to traditional Southern Democratic policies, the *Whig* was among the earliest of the bill's journalistic supporters. In early 1883, noting the presentation of the original Blair bill to the Senate, this newspaper hoped that it would be "favorably and speedily considered." As the debates proceeded, the *Whig* never failed to denounce those Southern Democrats who opposed federal aid, commenting that "the education of the masses will not be favored by the Democratic party, whose majorities come from the assemblage of ignorance and vice," labeling the southern Democratic opposition "barbarians of Bourbonism," and saying of them that "It is hard to teach old dogs new tricks." The *Whig* considered none of the objections raised to the bill as consequential and, in response to accusations that the South was coming as a "beggar for national alms" retorted that, on the contrary, federal aid was a means of getting back "some of the money that was extorted from us." Until 1887, the *Whig* evidenced confidence that the bill would not be allowed to die in the House of Representatives—it never indicated concern for a veto from President Cleveland—but its sanguinity rapidly declined in the face of the repeated failure of the measure to reach

[90]Birmingham, Alabama, *Age,* February 13, 1886; *see also Age-Herald,* December 19, 1889.

[91]Portsmouth, Virginia, *Enterprise,* December 18, 1887.

the floor of that chamber. Thus, the tendency toward disinterest in the Blair bill which characterized much of public sentiment in the late 1880's was characteristic of one of the bill's most ardent supporters.[92]

Spearheading much of Southern antipathy toward the Blair bill and federal aid generally was the Louisville, Kentucky, *Courier-Journal*. Under its brilliant editor, Henry Watterson, this newspaper took the lead in opposing carpet-bag influences, maintaining the rights of Negroes, and giving voice to a policy of "Democratic liberalism." The *Courier-Journal*, with the New Orleans *Times-Picayune*, had the largest daily and weekly circulation in the South throughout almost the entire decade.[93] With regard to federal aid, the *Courier-Journal* represented that segment of Southern opinion which considered such proposals as insulting, which had great faith in the ability of the South to support its institutions adequately without assistance, and which feared any extension of federal authority. "People must not rely upon the General Government to keep their common schools going. That process is pernicious in more ways than one." So wrote Watterson in 1882. Later, he declared his belief that any measures of this kind were Republican maneuvers "to add some additional levers to the political machine. Under such control the Bureau of Education would become a sink of foul corruption."[94] It is significant that the *Congressional Record* registers only twelve petitions from Kentucky groups for the entire decade, fewer than the number received from Maine, a state whose Senators were consistently hostile, during one session of Congress.

Something of an epitaph for the Blair bill appeared in another opposition newspaper, the Wilmington, Delaware, *Evening Journal*, as the Blair bill was about to be voted into oblivion in 1890. "Now, after twenty-five years of mistakes, after the South has recovered, after the Southern people have been ex-

[92]Richmond, Virginia, *Whig*, January 10, 1883; April 9, 14, 1884; February 11, 17, 18, 21, March 7, 1886.

[93]Mott, *American Journalism, op. cit.*, 361, 457-458.

[94]Louisville, Kentucky, *Courier-Journal*, March 16, 18, 1882; January 18, 1883.

hausting their millions to educate and improve the condition of the blacks, the Senator [Blair] and his party come to them with a measure that is offensive in its provisions and inadequate in its means."[95] Such a statement reflected a widespread and ever-growing antipathy in the South toward federal assistance of any kind.

New York City. "Every Democratic paper in New York [City] of any consequence has advocated this bill; the Herald, the Times, the Sun, the World . . . and the New York Post, I think, originally." So declared Senator Blair in the debate of 1890, indicating that it had been a characteristic of New York journals to switch their allegiance regarding federal aid from support to opposition. It would be unwise to accept Blair's assignment of partisan labels to that city's newspapers, and that which he attributed to those journals was largely untrue. Of the New York *Times* only could it be said that the original policy was one favorable to the Blair proposals. The *World* and the *Post*, on the contrary, were editorializing against federal aid to education before the Blair bill was under consideration by the Senate. The one avowedly Republican paper of consequence, the *Tribune*, was never a supporter of this legislation.

In New York City, where the journalistic discussion of this issue reached its peak, the newspapers were almost solidly opposed to the Blair bill, regardless of their political leanings. The lone supporter was the *Times*. This support, however, ceased after the debate of 1884, a development coincidental with that newspaper's break with the Republican party. Mugwump rather than Democratic, the *Times* gradually assumed the Democratic position relative to the Blair bill, and by 1890 its editors could write:

The vote on the Blair Educational bill in the United States Senate yesterday was a gratifying surprise. . . . The bill is dead, and there is no sort of doubt that the cold-blooded way in which it has been disposed was in a measure due to the weariness and disgust which Mr. Blair himself has produced by making such a hobby of it. . . . The

[95]Wilmington, Delaware, *Evening-Journal,* March 12, 1890.

bill was regarded as a nuisance to be got out of the way. . . . The perusal of [Blair's speeches] would be a penitential performance appropriate to this season [Lent]. . . .[96]

The other journals—the *Tribune*, then "the leading newspaper organ of the Republican party"; the *Sun;* and the enormously successful Pulitzer-owned *World*, liberal and independent; and a Tammany organ, the *Star*—consistently stood in opposition to the Blair bill.   All were agreed that the gravest objection to the bill was, in the words of the *Tribune*, that "it will teach the people . . . to look to the National Government for aid in discharging municipal duties."   The *Sun* called the measure "a deadly blow at the right of self-government . . . a fatal solvent of [the States'] independence."   And not even Republican newspapers challenged the *World's* assertion that "Mr. Blair's Educational bill seeks to use the surplus money's [sic] taken out of the pockets of the people unnecessarily and unjustly to establish a monster and monstrous system of national education which shall enormously increase the Federal patronage and turn the common schools into Republican missions."[97]

But it was the New York *Evening Post* which unquestionably led the journalistic opposition to the federal aid proposals of the 1880's. The *Post* was quoted throughout the country on this issue—it was generally recognized, apparently, that no other newspaper had exerted anything like the effort of the *Post* in studying and analyzing the Blair bill and its implications. This effort was the work of the *Post's* distinguished "moderate liberal" editor, Edward L. Godkin, under whom that newspaper became "the most inspiring force in American journalism."[98] According to Nevins, Godkin's *Post* was required reading for all intellectuals, newspaper men, and public officials and was subscribed to by a majority of the Congress.[99] President Cleve-

---

[96]New York *Times*, February 21, March 21, 1890; see also March 18, 20, 22, 1884; March 6, 1886; February 15, 16, 1888.
[97]New York *Tribune*, February 25, 1883; March 23, 1884.
   New York *Sun*, February 21, 23, March 14, 1890.
   New York *World*, March 17, 1882; April 1, 1884.
   New York *Star*, January 14, 1890.
[98]Allen Nevins, *The Evening Post: A Century of Journalism*, 545.
[99]*Ibid.*, 454.

land read the *Post* "faithfully, respected its views," and held Godkin in high regard.[100] The *Post* was, without doubt, "one of the most distinguished papers in America."[101]

Carl Schurz, who preceded Godkin as editor, had written editorials opposing federal aid to the common schools in 1883, considering such a procedure "an interference with the functions and self-reliance of the States." Godkin continued this policy, carrying it to such lengths that perhaps he, as much as any other one man, can be credited with effecting the defeat and the disappearance from national consideration of federal aid proposals.

The case against the Blair bill developed by the *Post*—which was presented in eleven editorials appearing during the debate of 1886, eight editorials in 1887 when no federal aid measure was on the Congressional docket, and in extensive reprints of these during 1888 and 1889—was based upon three assertions. First, said the *Post*, the South was constantly growing in local ability to cope with the problem of educational deficiency—"Every year will find her able to do more for education than the year before." Second, the argument of the bill's proponents that Southern need was acute was specious since, in many respects, Southern school systems, attendance records, and enrollment figures were equal to those of most and superior to those of some Northern states—"Illiteracy has been avoided in New England by a school system no better than that which many Southern States have, and which the rest can have without national aid and without unduly burdening the people." The *Post*'s third basic position was a belief that federal support of education would destroy local "self-reliance and self-respect" by inducing a relaxation of local and state efforts—"All the pleas for Federal aid proceed upon the assumption that such aid will be a good thing for the South. It is this assumption which we combat." This constituted the *Post*'s main line of argument, to which it returned again and again. The experience of the state of Connecticut with the proceeds of the sales of her Western Reserve

[100]Mott, *American Journalism, op. cit.,* 425 ff.
[101]*Ibid.,* 466.

land was cited: the *Post* maintained that the application of those moneys to public schools resulted in "a very striking deterioration" in popular support of education. Similarly, said the *Post*, the "mere passage of the Blair bill through one branch of Congress . . . had the effect to hinder the progress of the public-school system in South Carolina." The *Post* quoted from a letter on the subject which Woodrow Wilson had addressed to that paper, commenting upon a visit to the state legislature of Georgia in 1886. "It was evident," wrote Wilson, "that no increase in the State appropriation for public education would be voted so long as there was the least prospect of aid from Washington. . . . [There was] deliberate determination to enjoy the easy position of a beneficiary of the National Government to the fullest possible extent, rather than to be independent and support a good school system by its own unaided efforts." It is significant, in assessing the position and influence of the campaign of the *Post*, to note that it was not concerned over the issue of constitutionality, it made no accusations of political plotting nor did it raise gross spectres of centralization and bureaucracy, and no evidence exists that it argued from reasons of economy. On the contrary, it seems clear that the *Post*, i.e. Godkin, based its opposition to the Blair bill simply on a dispassionate, non-partisan belief in the measure's undesirability. This in itself was rare among newspapers who participated in the federal aid debate, and no journal approximated the sustained, vigorous, but totally impersonal quality that was characteristic of the entire *Post* series. Its influence, both in Congress and with the general public, was considerable, intelligent, and crucial.[102]

Thus, the 1880's—specifically the Blair bill—brought the federal aid question squarely to the forefront of much of American editorial thought. Any attempt to assess the potency of this journalistic expression in determining the legislative outcome is subject to challenge, but a few significant factors are worthy

[102]New York *Evening Post*, January 16, February 6, 27, March 1, 23, 1886; March 29, August 22, December 31, 1887. For the entire series of *Post* editorials on the Blair bill, see N. Y. Evening Post, *A Bill to Promote Mendicancy*, a reprint of all editorials on this subject which appeared during 1886 and 1887.

of note. Southern Senators acted largely in conformity with the sentiments expressed in Southern newspapers, generally supporting the measure until 1888, then, as the papers lost interest or followed the national trend towards disapproval, shifting their votes to the side of the opposition. On the other hand, only a few Senators from the unconcerned Far West opposed the bill, thus parting company with much of Western editorial opinion. Newspaper expressions, especially the writings of Godkin in the New York *Post*, were carefully studied and extensively cited in Senate debate; it is not inconceivable that many Senators who admitted a lack of conviction regarding this question were profoundly influenced by such statements. Undoubtedly, the very severity and concentration of editorial attack upon the Blair bill under Godkin's influence outweighed the less persuasive voices of the supporting journals. One cannot avoid the conclusion that with a Godkin favoring the bill the results might have been quite different.

· VI ·

THE BLAIR BILL—1882-1890: POLITICAL AND CONGRESSIONAL ACTIVITY; SIGNIFICANCE OF THE PROPOSED LEGISLATION

THE POLITICAL PARTIES

DURING the 1880's, the question of the fostering and support of public education lost none of the political coloration it had obtained in the previous decade. Both major parties and the burgeoning minor parties of the period found it desirable, from a sense of expediency or conviction, to note their devotion to the common schools. The political flavor of partisan commitments is indicated by the caustic Republican rebuke, "The ark of Democratic safety is ignorance,"[1] and by the answer in a Democratic catechism: "We are Democrats because we believe in the education of the masses . . . [and] favor the fostering and protection by State action, of common schools."[2]

The Republican Party

Two of the three Republican platforms for the Presidential campaigns of the 1880's were considerably more specific with regard to the relationship of the national government to education than had theretofore been the case. That of 1880 reaffirmed the previously proclaimed belief in the public schools and the prohibition of funds from "sectarian schools." While noting that "The work of popular education is one left to the care of

[1]Republican National Committee, *The Republican Campaign Text Book for 1884,* 76.
[2]S. S. Bloom, *Why We Are Democrats,* 188.

the several States," this platform in the first such statement by either major party, held that "it is the duty of the National Government to aid that work to the extent of its constitutional ability."[3] The platform of 1884, perhaps in the face of the Mugwump movement and increased Democratic strength, omitted all mention of education and returned to a zealous championship of states' rights. But, in its platform for 1888, the Republican party renewed its commitment to some form of federal aid in a statement full of conviction.

In a Republic like ours, where the citizen is the sovereign and the official the servant, where no power is exercised except by the will of the people, it is important that the sovereign—the people—should possess intelligence. The free school is the promoter of that intelligence which is to preserve us as a free nation; therefore the State or nation, or both combined, should support free institutions of learning sufficient to afford to every child growing up in the land the opportunity of a good common school education.[4]

Republican chief executives continued to evidence deep concern for the restoration of Southern education. Hayes and Garfield, in office before the introduction of legislation designed to apply federal funds directly to educational support, repeatedly urged enactment of laws devoting the public lands to that purpose. Of the necessity for such legislation, a biographer quotes Garfield as saying in 1881, "I am going to keep that subject before me all the time," and attributes to him a deep urge favoring "national aid to public, and especially to Southern education."[5] The annual messages of Chester A. Arthur, however, included the most decisive and direct challenges to Congress on behalf of federal aid of any nineteenth century president. Fully aware of the difficulties, both constitutional and political, which accompanied such legislation, he nevertheless expressed deep faith in its efficacy and essentiality. In his first annual message, Arthur wrote:

[3]George D. Ellis, *Platforms of the Two Great Political Parties*, 51.
[4]*Ibid.*, 75.
[5]B. A. Hinsdale, *President Garfield and Education*, 174. See also James D. Richardson, *A Compilation of the Messages and Papers of the Presidents, 1789-1879*, VII, 626; *The Republican Campaign Text Book for 1880*, 187; and for *1882*, 74.

Although our system of government does not contemplate that the nation should provide or support a system for the education of our people. . . . there is now a special reason why, by setting apart the proceeds of its sales of public lands or by some other course, the Government should aid the work of education. . . . all that can be done by local legislation and private generosity should be supplemented by such aid as can constitutionally be afforded by the National Government.[6]

Arthur's second message went further; he was convinced that the status of illiteracy over the nation presented "a momentous question for the decision of Congress whether immediate and substantial aid should not be extended by the General Government . . . in behalf of education."[7] His subsequent annual messages reiterated this position in unmistakable terms.

As with the platform, so with the campaign of 1884. The Republican party apparently chose to restrain its emphasis on the issue of federal assistance. Thus, the only important reference to the question on the part of Republican campaigners was contained in the speech of acceptance by the Vice-Presidential nominee, General John A. Logan. "As I have heretofore maintained, in order to achieve the ideal perfection of a popular government, it is absolutely necessary that the masses should be educated. . . . A liberal school system should be provided for the rising generation of the South. . . ."[8] Logan's advocacy of federal aid legislation had been far more vigorous in the Senate chamber.

With the election of Benjamin Harrison in 1888, a Republican proponent of national educational support again occupied the Presidency. In accordance with the policy expressed in the platform of the party, Harrison, in his first annual message, carried the commitment of Republican presidents one step further.

No one will deny that it is of the gravest national concern that those who hold the ultimate control of all public affairs should have the necessary intelligence wisely to direct and determine them. National aid to education has heretofore taken the form of land grants. . . . I

[6]Richardson, *op. cit.*, VIII, 58.
[7]*Ibid.*, VIII, 144; see also VIII, 184 and 253.
[8]*The Republican Campaign Text Book for 1884*, 43.

do not think it can be successfully questioned when the form is changed to that of a direct grant of money from the public Treasury.[9]

Thus, beginning with Grant, Republican presidents had consistently followed the trend in the legislative development of federal aid to education until, with Harrison, the Executive was on record specifically in favor of direct monetary grants for that purpose. But this steady progression, traceable in Republican Presidential statements—from advocacy of a vague support of common schools, through requests for assignment of public land sale proceeds to public education, to assertion of belief in the constitutionality of direct appropriations for local schools—though generally expressed by the party leadership, was not characteristic of the party as a whole. Despite platforms, Presidential messages, and the pleadings of party leaders, a significant portion of the Republican party never subscribed to commitments to enact federal aid legislation. Thus, on this question, such statements cannot be considered as having been applicable to the entire party, though substantial unanimity among Republicans was twice obtained in the Senate.

The Democratic Party

The 1880's saw no change in the official Democratic policy with regard to federal aid to education from that which had been expressed during the previous decade. On the contrary, in many instances, the antipathetical position was reinforced. This was especially true of the platforms drafted for the 1880 and 1884 Presidential campaigns.

The Democrats of the United States, in convention assembled, declare, in their platform of 1880, "Opposition to centralization and to that dangerous spirit of encroachment which tends to consolidate the powers of all the departments in one, and thus to create, whatever be the form of government, a real despotism."

This statement also placed the party on record in favor of "common schools fostered and protected."[10] In 1884, the Democratic stand was made more emphatic.

[9]Richardson, *op. cit.,* IX, 54.
[10]Ellis, *op. cit.,* 47.

We favor . . . the separation of church and state, and the diffusion of free education by common schools, so that every child in the land may be taught the rights and duties of citizenship. . . . [But] We are opposed to all propositions which, upon any pretext, would convert the General Government into a machine for collecting taxes, to be distributed among the States, or the citizens thereof.[11]

The platform of 1888, when many Democrats perhaps fore-saw the early final defeat of the Blair bill and thus felt relieved of any necessity for commenting upon the federal aid issue, made no mention of education whatever. But in 1892, when the struggle for federal assistance was over, the Democratic plat-form contained a statement on education which might well serve as a summary of the party's official position from the Civil War to that time. In a special section dealing exclusively with education, the party leadership declared:

Popular education being the only safe basis of popular suffrage, we recommend to the several States most liberal appropriations for the public schools. Free common schools are the nursery of good gov-ernment, and they have always received the fostering care of the Democratic party, which favors every means of increasing intelli-gence. Freedom of education being an essential of civil and religious liberty as well as a necessity for the development of intelligence, must not be interfered with under any pretext whatever. We are opposed to State interference with parental rights and rights of conscience in the education of children as an infringement of the fundamental Democratic doctrine that the largest individual liberty consistent with the rights of others insures the highest type of Amer-ican citizenship and the best government.[12]

Aside from the platforms, however, Democratic spokesmen apparently considered it either inexpedient or unnecessary, out-side Congressional debates, to comment upon the question of federal support for education. That it did not loom large in the party's campaign strategy was evidenced by the fact that the subject was completely ignored by the various *Democratic Campaign Textbooks* of the period. The Democratic adminis-tration of Grover Cleveland was equally notable for its silence on the question. While Cleveland has been credited with great

11*Ibid.*, 58.
12*Ibid.*, 84-85.

faith in the free common school, the promotion of education through federal activity was not among his administrative concerns. On the contrary, his regard for the maintenance of states' rights and his reliance upon a strict interpretation of the Constitution—"The preservation of the partitions between proper subjects of Federal and local care and regulation is of such importance under the Constitution . . . that no consideration of expediency or sentiment should tempt us to enter upon doubtful ground"[13]—indicate the strong likelihood that, had the Blair bill passed the House of Representatives in 1886 or 1888, a Presidential veto would have been employed. Indeed, President Barnard of Columbia College observed of Cleveland that "it is a comfort to think we have a President who is at once a man of sense and a man of nerve, and who will not fail to crush this vicious creation of political craft and political folly under his heel."[14]

While there were, as Senate votes indicated, many Democrats who were not in complete sympathy with the official party policy of ignoring the educational problem and who proclaimed themselves in favor of some form of federal aid, there were few who did not at the same time express fear of the possibility of federal control. Southern Democratic state governors, as a rule, joined in the public demand from that section for federal support of education, but only if that support were "stripped and freed from every possible condition of Federal supervision or control" and appropriated to states for use under state laws exclusively.[15] Another, and equally vocal wing of the party, however, despite concern that local initiative in school support be encouraged, bitterly coupled Republican agitation for federal aid with Republican protectionism. That party's tariff policies, these Democrats maintained, had produced a national treasury so overflowing as to require "schemes for extravagant and useless expenditure." It was this situation, said they, which led Republican protectionists to attempt to "sap the independence and

---

[13]Albert E. Bergh (ed.), *Letters and Addresses of Grover Cleveland*, 162.
[14]F. A. P. Barnard, *The Critic, op. cit.*, 266.
[15]U. S. Bureau of Education, *Report of the Commissioner of Education for the Year 1887-1888*, 168.

stifle the rising power and willingness of the South to maintain its local schools by offering largesses from the Public Treasury."[16]

Thus, the decade of the 1880's produced no fundamental change in official major party policies with regard to the federal aid question. Both parties, however, did make their positions clearer, unmistakably reaffirming previous commitments. While Republican leadership, to a considerable degree, moved in accord with the evolution of the idea of direct federal support, Democratic policy-makers held fast to their traditional position. It is of interest to note that, while Republican platforms eschewed any further mention of federal aid until 1920, the stand which the Democratic party took was reversed by its platform of 1912 in which federal support of vocational education was urged.

The Minor Parties

The minor political parties, like the farmer and labor organizations, were concerned with remedial action in areas more acutely touching pay envelopes and prices than that of common school improvement. The American Independent National or Greenback party, demanding the prohibition of child labor and the support of educational institutions, conceived of federal aid as merely one feature of the "amelioration of the condition of labor."[17] Compulsory education and federal support thereof continued to be basic planks in the platforms of the Prohibition party and similar sentiments were proclaimed by the Socialist-Labor party, which, however, did not participate in a Presidential election until 1892. While adherents of such political organizations were doubtless in complete sympathy with the Blair proposal, though some must have considered it inadequate, the fact of their support was of no consequence in affecting either the introduction of such legislation or its fate in the Congress. To some extent, albeit temporarily, the educational policies of the "radical" parties had been preempted by the Republican party.

---

[16]William L. Wilson, *The Tariff*, 7.

[17]Thomas Hudson McKee, *The National Conventions and Platforms of All Political Parties: 1789 to 1900*, 216.

THE BLAIR BILL DEBATES[18]

Finally, under the brave and persistent advocacy of Hon. Henry W. Blair, of New Hampshire, seconded by a noble demonstration in behalf of the common school by the most distinguished Senators from the ex-Confederate States, in a debate beyond comparison the most memorable for broad and patriotic sentiment of any since the close of the civil war, the Senate, at three successive sessions of Congress, passed a bill that would have advanced the entire condition of affairs in the South twenty years.[19]

So wrote the Reverend A. D. Mayo, one of the best informed, most distinguished, and most energetic lay champions of federal aid in 1893. His praise for the general excellence and sincerity of the Blair bill debates has been echoed by many, both contemporaries and latter-day historians. Unquestionably, these debates rank among the finest ever held in Congress on any legislation dealing with educational affairs.

Before discussing the debates and the succession of votes in the Senate on this proposal, a few general remarks are in order. In the first place, despite the fact that this was specifically educational legislation, questions that transcended considerations peculiar to education were the constant primary concern of the Senators. As before, and since, the debates on the Blair bill reflected an all-pervading and acute anxiety regarding constitutionality, respect for states' rights, the potential of federal control over local institutions, and the loss of local independence in their administration. Second, despite officially declared partisan

[18]*Congressional Record*, 48:1 (1884) 36, 758, 1744, 1999-2032, 2061-72, 2099-112, 2145-53, 2204-15, 2242-55, 2282-92, 2329-42, 2368-76, 2460-71, 2506-16, 2534-57, 2580-98, 2629-49, 2678-2724. 49:1 (1886) 130, 448, 501, 1171, 1197, 1207, 1237-83, 1286, 1318, 1335-45, 1432-40, 1468-85, 1559-68, 1596-1610, 1635-45, 1691-1703, 1724-39, 1766-82, 1917-27, 1904, 1939-59, 1989-2001, 2026-38, 2082-2105. 50:1 (1888) 27, 86, 127, 133, 143, 171, 196, 204, 263-8, 295-6, 347, 379, 422, 442, 511, 542, 567, 625, 653, 665, 669, 698, 709, 734, 739, 790, 833, 868, 899, 905-7, 972, 981, 1012, 1022, 1046, 1076, 1088, 1139-49, 1181-2, 1212, 1223. 51:1 (1890) 100, 213, 771, 1067, 1084, 1160, 1169, 1199, 1276, 1386, 1435, 1478, 1535-8, 1647, 1721, 1757-61, 1864, 1934, 2074-82, 2146-8, 2153, 2190, 2232, 2291, 2305, 2236-42, 2382-92, 2429-36, 2468-2639.

[19]A. D. Mayo, "Robert Charles Winthrop and the Peabody Education Fund for the South," *Report of the Commissioner of Education for the Year 1893-94*, I, 763.

positions with regard to federal participation in education, the voting on the Blair bill and the leadership in debate showed a wholesale disregard for party lines—i.e. in the Senate, support for the bill was led, over the entire period, by nine Republicans and eleven Democrats, while the opposition leadership was composed of twelve Democrats and five Republicans. Third, as evidence of the relative nonpartisanship and sincerity which characterized the debates, much of the most severe criticism of the Blair bill came from Senators who were wholeheartedly in favor of the federal aid principle, and who ultimately voted for the bill, but who felt that it contained important inadequacies. In the fourth place, although taken together these debates can only be characterized as of the highest caliber, there was a noticeable gradual diminution in thoroughness and quality as successive considerations of the bill were held, until, in 1890, Senatorial discussion was relatively cursory and lacking in the impassioned tenor of the earlier debates. The sense of urgency with which the bill was first considered had disappeared; there was apparently a resignation on the part of the measure's supporters to inevitable defeat and this final debate seems to have been largely one in which Senators wished merely to place themselves "on the record." Contributing to this, as the fifth point, was the growing potency of the argument that the South had made remarkable strides toward economic recovery since the war and that federal aid, particularly after 1886, was neither needed nor desired. Finally, and no overview of these debates would be complete without it, tribute must be paid to the magnificent leadership, prodigious effort, and complete sincerity of Senator Blair. It is doubtful that American education has had, at any time, so devoted a champion in the national legislature.

It is possible to synthesize and summarize the four debates, which involved reiterations and reinterpretations of previously declared positions as well as arguments newly developed as a result of the Blair proposal. That which follows is an attempt to present such a synthesis schematically and in a manner which represents, insofar as possible, the relative importance of the various arguments offered by the bill's proponents and opponents.

PRO

1. A literate electorate, hence an adequate, effective school system throughout the nation is essential to the maintenance of democratic government. "I ask the Senator from Texas, or the Senator from Maryland or the Senator from any State in this Union to answer the question I have put every time when this constitutional doctrine has been discussed, namely, if the National Government be a government republican in form, and it has imposed upon it the duty to guaranty a government republican in form to the State, and the State neglects to educate the child, and the parent neglects to educate the child, and the child, the sovereign, becomes an ignoramus, and thereby by your own proposition incapable of self-government, is or is not the duty imposed on the nation in that case of last resort to educate the child?" (Blair—1888) The presence of widespread illiteracy is a constant source of peril to the democratic institutional structure. Furthermore, the "unknown margin of ignorance" which exists among those persons who stand above the minimum literacy requirements of the states "but below the true standard of competency and educational qualification for the duties of citizenship" cannot be overlooked. "I for one find it impossible to sleep in peace over this volcano." (Blair—1884)

CON

1. Legislation of this kind will undermine, not strengthen, the foundations of democratic government. It will result in the development among the states of a sense of dependence upon the federal government. "If parents and communities are relieved of all responsibility and expense in the education of their children they will feel less interest in their education." (Saulsbury, Delaware—1884)

PRO

2. Federal aid to education is unquestionably constitutional. In view of the crucial importance of an educated electorate, the "general welfare" clause cannot possibly exclude education. Furthermore, the fact that each child holds national, as well as state, citizenship, entitles the national government to make provision that he be trained for the responsibilities of that citizenship.

3. The history of Congressional activity demonstrates the existence of ample precedent for legislation of this character—i.e. the Ordinances of 1785 and 1787, the Morrill act, etc., "The lawyer who can draw a distinction between the granting of one-sixteenth section . . . to aid in the cause of education and the grant-

CON

2. No constitutional authority exists for legislating in support of education. "I deny that the common schools of these United States are within the jurisdiction of the Congress or the Government of the United States." (Coke, Texas—1884) "The words 'provide for the common defense and general welfare of the United States' are a qualification of the taxing power. . . . Congress, at least by this clause, has not power to 'provide for the common defense and general welfare.' How far it can do this is determined by subsequent clauses. Whatever it has power to do under such clauses, this clause authorizes it to impose taxes to pay for." (Bayard, Delaware—1884) "If the constitutional power exists in Congress to levy and collect taxes from the people for the purpose of partially defraying the expense of public schools in the States, it exists for the purpose of paying the entire cost of the public school of all the States whenever Congress shall choose to exercise it." (Coke, Texas—1884)

3. To equate this measure with earlier legislation granting lands in support of education is invalid. The Constitution specifically gives Congress authority to dispose of the public domain, but no such authority exists to appropriate money for education. "The advocates of the pending bill argue that if Congress can

PRO

ing of money equivalent to that land can refine more than I am able to do and more than I ever want to do in the Senate of the United States." (Jones, Florida—1884) Furthermore, the areas which contain the least illiteracy are those which have, in the past, received the most assistance from the national government. Thirdly, there is no worthier cause to which the surplus in the national treasury could be devoted.

CON

thus apply the public domain or its proceeds it can tax the people to raise a fund for like application. This, to my mind, is a non-sequitur." (Maxey, Texas—1886) Existence of a treasury surplus which might be applied to education means that revision of the tax system is required—if the federal government were run more economically, the needy states would then have sufficient resources to build adequate educational systems independently. "Mr. President, we will help ourselves if you will take your hands off of us. . . . if you will quit taxing us to support your factories in the North. . . . If you will quit taking public lands to build railroads . . . we will help ourselves." (Vance, North Carolina—1884) The South is most concerned about the "iniquities of the present tariff system of taxation, which it is the main object of the Republican advocates of this bill to maintain and perpetuate by squandering money on anything that is plausible." (Beck, Kentucky—1884)

4. This legislation is "the logical consequence and true conclusion of the war." It is the duty of the federal government, having enfranchised the Negroes, to provide them with the means to exercise that franchise wisely. "The danger is to the whole Union from the exercise of the ballot in the hands of those new-made citizens." (Brown, Georgia—1884)

4. The installation of a system of federal participation in local education will inevitably introduce party politics into the schools. For the South, this would become "the most potent means of inciting anew and keeping alive race issues now being so happily solved." (Coke, Texas—1888) Enactments of this nature are measures of "agrarianism and

PRO

In addition, the Negro population is not now as industrious, "tractable" or disciplined as before; without definite provisions for the improvement of their status, the Negroes constitute an ever-growing menace. The Blair bill is "the first step and most important step that this Government has ever taken in the direction of the solution of what is called the race problem." (Lamar, Mississippi—1884)

5. Although the greater part of the benefits of the bill would accrue to the South, it is designed to meet, albeit inadequately, the educational needs of the entire nation. "I do not think there are sittings or accommodations of any kind, no matter how primitive and inexpensive, for one-half our school population. We have now less than 300,000 teachers and an average of more than 66 pupils for each. We require at least 200,000 more, and both the professional standard and the pecuniary compensation of the body as a whole should be very much raised." (Blair—1884) The proportion of illiteracy in the North must not be overlooked. "There is no one of the national elections, so closely contested as they are, which is not at the disposal of the ignorant vote in any one of the great cities of the North." (Blair—1884) Only by making use of the revenues of the national government can the delinquent states be improved,

CON

communism." "You will invite the men who are restless to-day, the labor organizations and other associations of men, to come here and say, "You bestowed your charity to relieve illiteracy; bestow your charity upon us to relieve us; we are out of employment." (Saulsbury, Delaware—1886)

5. The need for federal aid to education does not exist. "The Republic seems to be about as sound and as strong as if every man in it had been able to read and write." (Morgan, Alabama—1886) The South is slowly and consistently improving and increasing its educational facilities. These debates have been instrumental "in creating and awakening a spirit of shame which long ago began to apply a corrective . . . . I believe nothing in the situation today warrants, in order to get this money into Southern treasuries, that we shall vote eighteen or twenty million dollars to Northern States." (Spooner, Wisconsin—1890) It is unjust to tax the states with well-established school systems for the benefit of states whose systems are less advanced. "I have no right to tax the people of Florida to sustain public institutions in Alabama." (Morgan, Alabama—1886)

PRO

yet "Even after the distribution is made the Northern child will receive (combining the national and State assistance in one sum) $3 where the Southern child will receive $1 for his education . . . ." (Blair—1884) Southern states are unable to tax further for educational purposes.

6. The bill is so designed that the earlier federal grants are larger and the required state contributions smaller; if states are forced to match the federal appropriations in toto from the start, many will be unable to qualify for aid. Presumably, as states grow more prosperous and contribute more to education, the federal grants will decrease. Furthermore, the federal funds must be appropriated according to illiteracy—the money must be spent where the need exists.

7. Any bill of this nature requires that the federal government impose certain conditions. This, too, is supported by precedent (i.e. Morrill Act). "If Congress had the power to make the appropriation, Congress had the power to follow that appropriation and direct the application." (Sherman, Ohio—1884) The conditions herein imposed are ample —no state will receive federal funds until they are fulfilled— legitimate, and necessary. The power of the federal government to "investigate" is a sufficient guarantee against abuse of

CON

6. Unless the states receiving aid are required to match the federal grants from the outset, local initiative will be destroyed. States will "put out their children to nurse to the General Government. . . . This bill is a premium to every State desiring to receive this bounty to return as many illiterate children as it can, in order to magnify the amount it shall get." (Plumb, Kansas—1884) The only equitable method of appropriation is according to total population, not illiteracy.

7.a. The conditions imposed by this bill are inadequate. "I am not satisfied that if this money were placed in their [Southern] hands it would be properly used for the education of all classes of the people of those States. . . . I do not think the United States when they come to deal with this matter ought to trust the settlement of important questions that grow out of this new policy to the action of the people of the Southern States, because the force of prejudice, the force of education, is so strong and potent. . . ." (Sherman, Ohio—1884)

PRO

the grants within the states. Inasmuch as states can reject the grants, federal control is not imposed, but may be accepted.

8. This bill involves a congressional commitment only for a set limited period. It "is entitled a bill for temporary aid. It has no purpose—so far as I know there is no purpose on the part of any one interested in the enactment of the bill into law that the aid shall be permanent. . . . I myself am one of those who would be very reluctant indeed to see the school system of the United States become permanently dependent upon aid from the General Government." (Blair—1886)

CON

Senator Sherman "will pardon me for saying in the same spirit that I could not trust him to control it." (Butler, South Carolina—1884)

b. This proposal imposes too many conditions on the recipient states: the elements of the curriculum, the amounts to be raised in the states, and the manner in which the money shall be spent —i.e. for equalization. "If you grant for an instant that the National Government has the right to make one single condition you grant the power in the National Government to control the school system absolutely in all the States." (Vest, Missouri—1884) By the Constitution, states have no "power to yield their jurisdiction" in this area, thus cannot accept the aid with conditions of the nature prescribed by the bill.

8. A commitment to appropriate for a ten year period is financially unsound and will destroy the end the bill is designed to serve. "The very safety of our financial system depends upon annual appropriations made according to the amount of money that we have collected annually from the various sources of revenue." (Sherman, Ohio—1884) Furthermore, "if you inflate the school system in a State by this artificial aid which lasts but a short time . . . you establish in that State an expensive system beyond the means of any State,

PRO   CON

and when the artificial stimulant is drawn away, your State capacity is not sufficient to keep up the system." (Maxey, Texas— 1884) Finally, it is unrealistic to maintain that aid of this sort will be temporary; the pressure for its continuance will be too strong to permit its cessation.

9. Public opinion is so decidedly favorable to this bill that Congress cannot ignore the nation-wide demand that it be passed. Since it was first introduced, "the measure has been generally and thoroughly discussed throughout the whole country, and probably public sentiment is more largely in favor of this bill than was ever known to be the case with any other of like importance in the history of American legislation." (Blair—1886)

9. The public has not expressed itself in favor of this measure sufficiently to warrant the passage of legislation so drastic. As to the expressions of public sentiment which have been received by Congress, "Any body will sign petitions and write letters in favor of education and schools. How many . . . know or care whether the authority to furnish the money to carry on these schools is in the States or in the Federal Government? And unless they had considered and understood this question, of what value are their petitions and letters to us in determining our duty on this subject?" (Reagan, Texas—1890)

The voting on the Blair bill is indicated by the accompanying chart. Votes were taken in the Senate on each of the four occasions on which the bill had been debated; the first three votes (1884, 1886, 1888) were votes of final passage, but the last (1890) was on the "engrossment and third reading" of the bill. Rejection of the bill at this stage of parliamentary procedure was tantamount to defeat of the bill, inasmuch as such a vote registered the Senate's refusal to consider it further. This explains the lone negative vote from New Hampshire in 1890, since Blair switched his vote in order to be in a position to move for the reconsideration of the bill. Such a motion was never placed before the Senate.

Perhaps the most striking feature of the voting record was the marked increase in the number of opposition votes in 1888. The general change in attitude toward the Blair bill which appeared after 1886 was reflected in the vote of 1888 at which time many Senators previously favorable were moved to oppose the bill. In addition, several Senators who had previously refrained from voting were constrained to register their opposition. This developing antagonism appeared among Senators from all sections of the country, but most notably among Southerners. While the favorable votes from the Northeast and the Far West in 1888 exceeded those of 1886, it was only from the Far West that a continually increasing favorable vote throughout the decade was registered.

Substantial majorities of both parties voted in favor of the bill, however, in 1884 and 1886, which meant, on the part of the Democratic Senators, a refusal to accept the official party position. In all four votes a majority of Republicans remained favorable to the Blair bill, though the extent of that majority was constantly lessened. Only with the vote of 1890 was there an actual majority of Democratic Senators registered in the opposition columns. Thus, a summary of the four votes involves a curious paradox: while neither party mustered a majority of its members in opposition to the bill until 1890, both parties showed a consistent tendency to repudiate the principles inherent in the bill as the successive votes were taken. Unanimity within party ranks was most nearly achieved by the Republicans in 1884, but it was not approximated among Democrats at any time.

Partisan affiliation should not, however, be overemphasized in analyzing and assessing the fate of the Blair bill in the Senate. While for some members of both parties this was assuredly the controlling factor, most Senators—if the debates and the disregard of such affiliations in voting are credited—were governed by honest conviction and sincere concern for the public interest as they interpreted it. There is indication, too, that these motivations outweighed the manifestations of local public sentiment

THE BLAIR BILL—SUMMARY OF THE VOTING IN THE SENATE: 1884 TO 1890

Legend: Voting is indicated by states, thus the maximum number of votes on the bill from any one state was eight (two per state in each of the four sessions during which the Blair bill was voted upon). A "D" indicates a Democratic vote, an "R" indicates a Republican vote.

	Pro			*States*	*Con*			
1890	1888	1886	1884		1884	1886	1888	1890
				NORTHEAST AND MIDDLE SEABOARD				
R	R		R	Connecticut	R		R	R
			R	Maine		R R	R R	R R
R R	R R	R	R R	Massachusetts				
R	R R	R	R R	New Hampshire				R
				New Jersey			D	D
R	R	R R	R	New York			R	R
	R R			Pennsylvania				
				Rhode Island			R	R R
R R	R	R	R R	Vermont				
7	9	5	9		1	2	6	8
				SOUTH				
D	D	D	D	Alabama	D		D	D
	D D	D D	D	Arkansas				D R
R				Delaware	D D	D	D D	D
D	D D	D	D D	Florida				
D	D D	D	D D	Georgia				
		D	D	Kentucky			D D	D
	D	D D	D	Louisiana				
				Maryland	D	D	D	D D
D	D D	D D	D	Mississippi				D
				Missouri		D	D	D D
	D	D D	D	North Carolina				
D	D D		D	South Carolina	D		D	
		D	D	Tennessee	D	D	D D	D D
				Texas	D D	D D	D D	D D
D D	D D	D D	D	Virginia				
		D	D	West Virginia			D D	D D
8	15	16	14		8	6	14	16
				MIDDLE WEST				
				Kansas		R R	R R	R R
R	R	R R	R R	Illinois			R	R
		D	R	Indiana			D D	D D
R R	R R	R	R	Iowa				
R R	R R	R R	R	Michigan				
			R	Minnesota			R R	R
R	R	R R	R	Nebraska				
	D	D		Ohio	D			D R
	R	R R	R R	Wisconsin			R	R R
6	8	11	9		1	2	8	10
				FAR WEST				
R D	R D			California	R			
R	R R	R R		Colorado				R
R	R			Nevada		R	R	R
				North Dakota				R
R R	R R	R R	R	Oregon				
R R				South Dakota				
R R				Washington				
10	7	4	1		1	1	1	3
31	39	36	33	*GRAND TOTALS*	11	11	29	37

in directing senatorial activity, as, for example, when Far Western Senators increasingly supported the bill despite the indifference or disapproval which was being expressed in their home
states.

There remains unanswered the question: Why did the Blair
bill fail to be enacted? An explanation must be couched on two
planes—it must note the complete inactivity of the House of
Representatives with regard to the Blair bill, and it must attempt
to clarify the factors which caused that chamber and the Senate
opposition to act as they did. What, then, were the forces
which effectively blocked the passage and enactment of the
Blair bill?

During the three Congresses in which the Senate passed the
Blair bill, the House of Representatives contained a Democratic
majority. Senator Blair claimed that, although two-thirds of the
members of the House were sympathetic to his proposal, an organized minority under Speaker John G. Carlisle of Kentucky
continually blocked consideration of the bill by that body. The
Speaker was accused, by Blair and others, of "fixing" the House
Committee on Education, of packing it with representatives
unfavorable to the federal aid idea.[20] Thus, when bills identical
to the Blair bill were sent to the House committee, that committee either reported back adversely on such bills or recommended the passage of other bills utterly inconsistent with the
basic policies advanced by the Blair bill. This was done deliberately, according to Blair, "for the purpose of killing the bill."
It was this situation which led Blair to attribute the defeat of the
bill to the machinations of one man, the Speaker, and it is important to note that he represented one of the Southern states
which from the outset had been least sympathetic to the proposal of federal assistance.

But any assessment of the underlying causes of the bill's defeat must go beyond parliamentary obstructionism. A prominent Northern educator, J. C. Hartzell, and an even more re-

---

[20]U. S. Bureau of Education, *Circular of Information No. 3, 1887*, 185-71.
See also *Journal of Education*, Boston, "Congress and National Aid," 23:41,
January 21, 1886.

nowned Southern leader, J. L. M. Curry, agreed that the chief factor which contributed to the defeat of the Blair bill was Southern reaction and resentment. Curry suspected that fear of the difficulty of controlling more educated Negroes and the potential upsetting of the traditional patterns of race relationships was the major cause of Southern opposition.[21] Hartzell, calling Southern rejection of national aid "the supreme folly," stated that "The chief factor against the best interests of the republic in that congressional struggle was Southern political bourbonism. . . ."[22] Both men joined Blair in attributing to Catholic opposition a large share of the credit for blocking full consideration of the bill. In addition to these, the very real economic recovery characteristic of the South in the 1880's, while in no sense producing a resource adequate to the educational needs of that region, lent strength to the other arguments advanced against the bill and contributed to the defection of Southern support. Finally, Southern reluctance to accept completely the basic public school idea, the region's inability to recognize the validity and essentiality of the principle of educational equalization, was a fundamental barrier. In Schlesinger's words, "At most, education was regarded in the South as an opportunity for the individual child and not as a civic obligation" until after 1900.[23]

[21]Merle Curti, *The Social Ideas of American Educators*, 272-273.

[22]J. C. Hartzell, "The Problem of Education in the Southern States," *Methodist Review*, 64:46-49, January, 1892.

[23]Arthur M. Schlesinger, *The Rise of the City: 1878-1898*, 166.

An interesting thesis bearing upon this matter was advanced by N. H. R. Dawson, Commissioner of Education from 1886 to 1889. In the Introduction to Frank W. Blackmar's *The History of Federal and State Aid to Higher Education*, published in 1890, Dawson wrote:

"One of the strongest inferences that may be drawn from this investigation is that in nearly every instance the foremost desire of the people has been for colleges and universities, rather than for schools of a lower grade. It was the opinion of the colonists and of the later settlers of the West and South that primary and secondary schools were essentially dependent for their existence upon higher institutions. This principle is borne out by the facts, for, then as now, wherever the best colleges and universities are, there will be the best grade of primary and secondary schools." Therefore, concluded Dawson, "to build up and strengthen higher learning is the safest plan for insuring the perpetuity of primary and secondary schools." 4-5.

THE SIGNIFICANCE OF THE BLAIR BILL AS A PHASE IN THE STRUGGLE TO OBTAIN FEDERAL AID FOR COMMON SCHOOLS: SUMMARY

1. The 1880's, as a period in the development of federal aid policies, was completely and exclusively dominated by the Blair bill. As such the period represents not only the climax of the nineteenth century struggle to obtain federal aid for the common schools, but also in a very real sense the beginning of current activity in this area.

2. The Blair bill was, and is, significant as stimulating the first serious consideration of the following provisions:

   a. Monetary aid, direct and temporary, for the common schools.

   b. Distributions of federal funds according to illiteracy ratios.

   c. Appropriations governed by the extent of local efforts for education—the "matching" principle.

   d. Aid to the public common schools only, excluding denominational schools from the benefits of the act, designed in so far as possible to equalize educational opportunities.

   e. Administration of grants by states and local officials within a framework of certain general federal requirements and restrictions.

3. Public pressure in its behalf reached proportions never before approximated for any national educational legislation.

4. For the first time, the educational profession, in an organized way and on a national scale, led the fight outside of Congress for federal aid. A sizable minority, including most college and university officials, disapproved of the bill, and, while opposition within the profession never became organized, it was extremely influential. Educational publications did not, however, measure up to the demands of the situation in their coverage or analysis of the proposed legislation.

5. Protestant denominations were forced into greater activ-

ity on this issue than heretofore. Unlike the Catholic Church, whose opposition to any federal aid continued unabated, the Protestant leadership was decidedly disunited as to the desirability of the Blair bill. Many Protestants agreed with the Catholic position that such legislation was prejudicial to the effective promulgation of "positive religious teaching."

6. Organized agriculture, while proclaiming extreme interest in the maintenance and improvement of the common schools, did not establish a definite position with regard to the Blair bill nor did it engage actively in the campaign to effect its passage.

7. Organized labor evidenced more interest in federal aid legislation during the 1880's than ever before—both the Knights of Labor and the American Federation of Labor resolved and petitioned regularly in behalf of the bill—but it is doubtful that its efforts were decisive.

8. Organized business, concerned during this period only with legislation definitely affecting its interests, played no part in the Blair bill controversy. With a few local exceptions, business was altogether silent on the question of federal aid to education.

9. The two major parties found it expedient, even essential, to declare definite official positions with regard to the relationship of the Federal Government to education. The decade was featured by continually more vigorous commitments—by the Republican party to the federal aid principle, by the Democratic party to states' rights and the preservation of local initiative—which reaffirmed previously published positions. Congressional performance, however, indicated extensive intraparty disagreement on this question.

10. Increased attention to federal aid by the nation's press was characteristic of the 1880's. Newspaper interest in the issue jumped markedly, especially in the South and in New York City; the extensive coverage and intensive analysis afforded this question by newspapers indicates the probability that they were far more influential than periodical publications in shaping public sentiment on this issue. The opposition press, centered in New York City, was an undeniably potent force in producing

the bill's defeat. With the general public, or perhaps leading it, the press followed the trend away from interest in and support of federal aid that was a national characteristic after 1886.

11. The Senate debates on the Blair bill were the most extensive, thorough, and able debates on educational legislation held in Congress to that time, if not, indeed, to the present. Succeeding debates reflected, however, the growing public disinterest in or lack of concern for federal aid which spread with increasing momentum after 1886.

12. The votes in the Senate on the Blair bill indicated:

    a. A substantial majority of both parties in favor of the bill in 1884 and 1886.

    b. A definite trend in both parties away from the principles inherent in the bill.

    c. A substantial return to conformity with partisan alignments by 1890.

    d. The non-existence of unanimity within either party at any time, though unanimity within Republican ranks was approximated in 1884 and 1886.

13. Though a scattering of federal aid measures was subsequently proposed in Congress, the Blair bill was the last such bill to be considered on the floor of either house until 1919, when the Smith-Bankhead bill was debated by the Senate.

· *VII* ·

CONCLUSION: OVERVIEW AND CONTEMPORARY SIGNIFICANCE

OVERVIEW OF THE PERIOD 1870-1890 IN TERMS OF THE CONSIDERATION AND DEVELOPMENT OF PROPOSALS FOR FEDERAL AID TO THE COMMON SCHOOLS

WHAT, then, were the dominant trends in political thought, professional sentiment and behavior, and organizational activity over this twenty-year period with regard to the issue of federal aid to common schools? And what implications do these findings hold for contemporary and possible future considerations of federal aid legislation? It is the function of this final chapter to present an overview of these findings, followed by an interpretation of their current significance.

1. This twenty-year period, and particularly the years 1884 to 1890, represents the greatest consolidation of Congressional effort to date in behalf of federal support for the common schools. Public and professional interest, however, have subsequently been more effectively mobilized on this issue, through increased professional concern, improved media of communication, and the more widespread acceptance of the necessity of common school education.

2. The period embraced a wide variety of proposals for handling federal aid:

    a. Outright national control of a system of education.

    b. Application of land sale proceeds to common schools.

    c. Application of specific federal revenues to common schools—i.e. liquor tax revenues, Patent Office income.

    d. Temporary direct federal grants to states for common schools, distributed according to population, total illiteracy, or school-age illiteracy, or as rewards for local effort.

3. During this period, political parties granted education official recognition as a *national* issue. This resulted in the development of definite partisan positions regarding the relationship of the Federal Government to public and private education: the Republican party officially and generally in favor of federal aid, the Democratic party officially and evermore generally opposed.

4. These two decades were featured by a widespread public awakening to the importance of education as a *national* concern. This was demonstrated by the increased coverage of the question of federal participation in education by the nation's press, by a vastly increased volume of public petitions to Congress bearing upon that issue, and by the growth of organized pressures to force Congressional action.

5. At the same time, the federal assistance question produced the beginnings of effective activity within the educational profession on more than a local or regional scale.

6. Throughout the 1870's and 1880's, the actions of many Congressmen on this issue were governed less than usual by party dogma or established political patterns, and considerably more than is customary by a recognition of the importance of the problem and sincere conviction as to the best means for meeting it. The consistent obstructionism to the Blair bill in the House of Representatives and the abandonment of the federal aid principle on the part of members of both parties, however, heralded the return to political tradition which contributed to the subsequent thirty-year absence of federal aid bills from Congressional calendars.

7. Consideration of the federal aid proposals that were advanced during this period established the impossibility of enacting any such legislation unless it authorized:

    a. Separate schools for white and Negro children.

b. Non-participation by denominational schools in the use of federal funds.

8. At no time during these twenty years was any one federal aid measure considered by both houses of Congress.

9. Perhaps most significant of all was the evidence, in Congressional and public debate, of the overpowering importance of considerations of constitutionality, states' rights, and centralization or federal control. Throughout the period and on a nation-wide scale, decided and determined opposition to national control of education was constantly manifested. To many, maintenance of local prerogative loomed far larger than educational improvement; to many more, independence from federal control was essential to that improvement.

THE CONTEMPORARY SIGNIFICANCE OF THE EARLY ATTEMPTS TO GRANT FEDERAL AID TO THE COMMON SCHOOLS

As mid-twentieth century Americans, facing a national educational problem even more acute and infinitely more urgent than that which confronted our nineteenth century predecessors —indeed, a problem which is crucial in its international as well as its national implications—what can we learn from that earlier experience? The history of those first attempts to enact federal legislation in support of the common schools demonstrates that certain very definite and basic factors in American tradition and behavior cannot be ignored in any future consideration of this issue.

These elements must, however, be viewed in the light of profound social and institutional change. While the agitation for federal aid in the 1870's and 1880's was to a large extent the direct result of the dislocation and devastation of the Civil War, increasingly it reflected growing awareness of the new demands of an industrial society. As the population became more mobile and sectional barriers disintegrated, as technical and technological training grew more essential, as the exigencies of urban living demonstrated the inadequacies of the educational patterns which had served agrarian society, there began to develop the concept of national responsibility for common school education. It was, therefore, recognition of this need to adjust to new economic and social conditions, as well as a realization that the political institutions of a democracy were endangered by educational deficiencies, which produced the public pressures to effect federal support of general education.

An analysis of the contemporary significance of these prior endeavors must also take into account the tremendous development of organized social pressure since 1890. One of the cardinal features of the activity with regard to federal participation in education from 1870 to 1890 was the lack of such pressure, indeed the apathy and unconcern, registered by groups which are today immensely powerful, active, and influential. Farmer and labor organizations during the late nineteenth century were, as has been noted, intensely preoccupied with the more immediate concerns of maintaining their existence and could hardly afford extensive participation in the federal aid debate. Their successors today are among the most active of the groups pressing for similar legislation. Likewise, business interests, by the 1880's not yet embarked upon the extensive integration of their power which characterizes contemporary American society, are now extremely conscious of their involvement in the problem of federal aid. So too with churches of all denominations and veterans' organizations of every shade—they cannot, like the Grand Army of the Republic in 1887, dismiss such issues as foreign to their aims and objects.

Despite these fundamental social changes, certain conclusions with regard to the period here under investigation can be adduced which hold significance and validity for contemporary and possible future attempts to enact similar, though of necessity far more extensive, federal legislation.

1. There exists among the American people a powerful and lasting tradition of states' rights and local prerogative, which is stronger perhaps in the area of educational affairs than anywhere else. This tradition has blinded the American public to the fact that federal participation in education is already a reality, that the question at issue therefore is not "Should the federal government participate?" but rather (in the words of the Educational Policies Commission of the National Education Association) "Can federal participation in education be kept within proper bounds and limits, or will it eventually swallow up all education in a system of centralized control and administration?"

Developments subsequent to the 1880's have indicated the possibility that such tradition is flexible in the face of emergency situations. The general acceptance of such federal activities as the National Youth Administration and the Civilian Conservation Corps demonstrated that, on the one hand, indirect federal support of common school education, and, on the other hand, federal provision of such education can operate without detriment to local initiative and independence. The performance of the 1870's and 1880's indicates, however, the unlikelihood of the passage of federal legislation designed to aid the common schools *directly* which embodies *any* federal controls other than the details of fiscal administration.

2. The educational profession during the 1870's and 1880's was extremely weak as a pressure group on the national level. The profession was utterly unable to unite in recognizing the urgent necessity of federal aid. No federal aid legislation is likely to be enacted without aggressive professional organization representing approximate solidarity of professional support for such legislation. It becomes the duty of the individual educator, therefore, to study critically the contemporary educational situation, to take a position with regard to the measures which are proposed to alleviate the problem, and to support *actively* those professional organizations which represent his position. Similarly, the organizations must exert ever more strenuous efforts to educate the profession relative to the urgencies of the current problem and the implications of proposed legislative remedial action. Only through such aggressive expression will the profession and the issue be accorded the respect and recognition which both deserve.

3. It is unwise to base appropriations for federal assistance to education on *total* population or *total* illiteracy within states.

Federal aid measures which (*a*) appropriate, for political purposes, where the need is slight, or (*b*) base such appropriations on numbers of persons the common schools will never reach are, to say the least, of doubtful validity. Federal aid must be applied where the need exists, with due regard for local resources, local efforts on behalf of education, and the national need for educational equalization.

4. There have been fundamental shifts in the attitudes of two important segments of society regarding federal aid to common school education. From the meager evidence available, it appears that the position of organized business during the 1880's was not one of hostility towards proposals of federal support for education. It would be rash to interpret the lack of concern which characterized most business interests as constituting approval but it is undeniable that certain groups of influential business leaders supported federal aid. Contemporary business activity in this area indicates a reluctance to accept large-scale federal participation in educational affairs and a reliance upon the ultimate effectiveness of local effort.

The pattern of opposition displayed by the Catholic Church has also undergone change. It is noteworthy that the continued opposition of the Catholic Church to any program of federal aid during the period 1870 to 1890 was tempered, at the time of the consideration of the Hoar bill, with a willingness to condone such legislation if parochial schools were allowed to participate in its benefits. Catholic antipathy to the Blair bill, however, reflected total rejection of that possibility in favor of outright denunciation of the entire program of federal support. The position of the Catholic Church today has thus returned to that which it held in 1870-1871: acceptance of the common school, refusal to make use of it, and demands for federal support of parochial education.

5. Similarly, there has occurred a shift in the official attitudes of the major political parties on the issue of federal aid to education. During the 1870's and 1880's, Republican party policy reflected a constantly strengthened commitment to the idea of federal support of common school education, while Democratic

party pronouncements proclaimed steadfast adherence to the strictest application of the states' rights doctrine in this area. The legislation of the 1930's, under a Democratic administration, and the policies enunciated in the recent platforms of both parties indicate that a direct reversal has evolved. Thus, it is today the Democratic party whose subscription to a program of federal aid to common school education is most definite, whereas official Republican policy expresses the traditional concern for local independence and fear of federal control. It must be noted, however, that in each period the behavior of congressmen of both parties has to a large degree demonstrated a refusal to accept official party policy on this question.

6. The experience of the 1870's and 1880's demonstrated the deep conviction within the American people of opposition to the use of public property for sectarian purposes. Certain groups in American society were then and continue to stand morally committed to social philosophies which preclude any genuine acceptance of federal participation in education. One such group is the Catholic Church, which cannot accept such federal participation in education in its fullest meanings and applications. Federal aid legislation cannot cater to such parochial commitments at the expense of the larger ends it is designed to serve, for to do so would mean their ultimate destruction. Such legislation, therefore, must proclaim unequivocal refusal to apply the benefits of federal aid to private schools of any description.

7. Another section of the American people is also unable to subscribe to a completely democratic implementation of a federal aid program. The position taken by those who maintain a morality of "white supremacy" was in the 1880's and is today regarded by some as rendering any program of federal aid ineffectual. Thus, many demand federal aid legislation which would be inapplicable to states in which racial segregation is a legally established practice. It must be recognized, however, that mandatory legislation will not produce reform of traditional social attitudes. A growing social consciousness, supported by the progressive tendencies of contemporary judicial decision, is gradually producing reform in the established patterns of race

relationships, notably in the area of educational equalization. However, it seems unwise to assume that this pervasive morality could be altered by the inclusion of mandates to that end in federal aid legislation. On the contrary, since universal education constitutes the surest and soundest means of attacking such attitudes, the exclusion of these sections of the country from the benefits of such legislation would militate against the successful operation of any federal aid program. Thus, as was demonstrated by the earlier attempts to enact such legislation, federal aid must be granted for use within the established patterns of social behavior characteristic of local communities. Indeed, it is not likely of enactment otherwise. This is admittedly a concession to an anti-democratic system of values, but one which is essential to the eventual elimination of those values and the continued implementation of American democracy. This is not to say that where states regularly apply public funds for the benefit of private institutions, federal moneys should be similarly distributed. (See 6) But the application of such funds for *public* use under *public* control, regardless of local patterns of social relationships, cannot but result in the enhancement of the general welfare. Only thus can the national responsibility be met.

8. Finally, there exists among the American people a traditional inability to accept the idea of social responsibility for education on a national scale. Today, as in the 1880's, the concept that the equalization of educational opportunity is a national problem is largely unrecognized. Until the public generally becomes aware of the dangers to democratic institutions which result from a deficiently educated electorate, federal aid to education is not likely to be realized or, at least, utilized with maximum effectiveness. Here the educational profession and the press must assume the greatest share of responsibility. The crucial essentiality of an educated American electorate to the nation and to the world forces us—educators and laymen alike—to exert every effort to prevent a repetition of the history here detailed.

BIBLIOGRAPHY

GENERAL REFERENCES

Appleton's Annual Cyclopedia and Register of Important Events of the Year(s) 1866 to 1890, New Series. New York, Appleton, 1867 to 1891.

Beard, Charles A. *The American Party Battle.* New York, Macmillan, 1928. 150 p.

Binkley, Wilfred E. *American Political Parties: Their National History.* New York, Knopf, 1945. 420 p.

Blackmar, Frank W. *The History of Federal and State Aid to Higher Education,* U. S. Department of Interior, Bureau of Education, Circular of Information No. 1, 1890, Washington, D. C., Government Printing Office, 1890. 343 p.

Boone, Richard G. *Education in the United States: Its History from the Earliest Settlements.* New York, Appleton, 1890. 402 p.

Butler, Nicholas Murray. *The Meaning of Education: Contributions to a Philosophy of Education.* New York, Scribners, 1915. 385 p.

The Catholic Encyclopedia; An International Work of Reference on the Constitution, Doctrine, Discipline and History of the Catholic Church, 15 vols. New York, Appleton, 1907-1912.

Cook, William A. *Federal and State School Administration.* New York, Crowell, 1927. 373 p.

Cooper, Thomas V. and Fenton, Hector T. *American Politics from the Beginning to Date.* Chicago, Brodix, 1882. 1058 p.

Cubberley, Ellwood P. *Public Education in the United States: A Study and Interpretation of American Educational History.* Boston, Houghton Mifflin, 1934. 782 p.

Cubberley, Ellwood P. *State and County School Administration: Vol. II, Source Book.* New York, Macmillan, 1915. 729 p.

Cubberley, Ellwood P. *State School Administration: A Textbook of Principles.* Boston, Houghton Mifflin, 1927. 773 p.

Curoe, Philip R. V. *Educational Attitudes and Policies of Organized Labor in the United States.* New York, Teachers College, Columbia University, 1926. 202 p.

Curti, Merle. *The Social Ideas of American Educators.* Report of the Commission on the Social Studies, Part X. New York, Scribners, 1935. 611 p.

Curtis, Francis. *The Republican Party: A History of Its Fifty Years' Existence and a Record of Its Measures and Leaders, 1854-1904.* New York, Putnam, 1904, 2 vols.

Dexter, Edwin G. *A History of Education in the United States.* New York, Macmillan, 1904. 656 p.

Douglas, Paul H. "The Development of a System of Federal Grants-in-Aid," *Political Science Quarterly,* 35:255-71, 522-44, 1920.

Ellis, George D. *Platforms of the Two Great Political Parties.* House of Representatives, Washington, D. C., Government Printing Office, 1920. 266 p.

Encyclopedia Brittanica: A New Survey of Useful Knowledge, 23 vols. London, Encyclopedia Brittanica, 1939.

Foster, Charles R., Jr. *Editorial Treatment of Education in the American Press.* Harvard Bulletins in Education, No. 21, Cambridge, Harvard University Press, 1938. 303 p.

Germann, George B. *National Legislation Concerning Education; Its Influence and Effect in the Public Land States East of the Mississippi River.* Ph.D. Thesis, Columbia University, New York, 1899. 194 p.

Graf, William and Trimble, South. *Platforms of the Two Great Political Parties: 1932-1944.* Washington, D. C., Government Printing Office, 1945. 459 p.

Greenleaf, Walter J. *Federal Laws and Rulings Affecting Land-Grant Colleges and Universities.* U. S. Office of Education Pamphlet No. 15, Washington, D. C., Government Printing Office, November 1, 1930. 13 p.

Judd, Charles H. *Research in the United States Office of Education.* Staff Study No. 19, Washington, D. C., Government Printing Office, 1939. 139 p.

Keesecker, Ward W. *Digest of Legislation Providing Federal Subsidies for Education.* U. S. Office of Education, Bulletin No. 8, Washington, D. C., Government Printing Office, 1930. 52 p.

Keith, John A. H. and Bagley, William C. *The Nation and Its Schools.* New York, Macmillan, 1920. 364 p.

Kleeberg, Gordon S. P. *The Formation of the Republican Party as a National Political Organization.* New York, n.p., 1911. 245 p.

Knight, Edgar W. *Public Education in the South.* Boston, Ginn, 1922, 482 p.

Logan, Edward B. (ed.). *The American Political Scene.* New York, Harpers, 1936. 264 p.

McKee, Thomas Hudson. *The National Conventions and Platforms of All Political Parties: 1789 to 1900.* Baltimore, Friedenwald, 1900. 402 p.

Mahoney, Robert H. *The Federal Government and Education: An Examination of the Federalization Movement in the Light of the Educational Demands of a Democracy.* Ph.D. Dissertation, Washington, D. C., Catholic University of America, 1922. 80 p.

Monroe, Will S. *Bibliography of Education.* New York, Appleton, 1897. 202 p.

Moore, Ernest Carroll. *Fifty Years in American Education.* Boston, Ginn, 1917. 96 p.

Mott, Frank Luther. *American Journalism: A History of Newspapers in the United States Through 250 Years: 1690 to 1940.* New York, Macmillan, 1941. 772 p.

Mott, Frank Luther. *A History of American Magazines.* Cambridge, Harvard University Press, 1938. 3 vols.

National Advisory Committee on Education. *Federal Relations to Education: Part I—Committee Findings and Recommendations; Part II—Basic Facts.* Washington, D. C., National Capital Press, 1931. Part I—140 p., Part II—448 p.

National Education Association of the United States, Educational Policies Commission. *Federal Activities in Education.* Washington, D. C., 1939. 151 p.

National Education Association of the United States, Educational Policies Commission. *Federal-State Relations in Education.* Washington, D. C., March, 1945. 47 p.

National Education Association of the United States, Educational Policies Commission, and American Council on Education, Problems and Policies Committee, *Source Book on Federal-State Relations in Education.* Washington, D. C., National Education Association, June, 1945. 159 p.

National Education Association of the United States. *Federal Laws Relating to Education.* Washington, D. C., National Education Association, Division of Research, 1945. 66 p.

National Education Association of the United States. *Federal Support for Education: The Issues and the Facts.* Research Bulletin of the National Education Association, Vol. 15, No. 4, Washington, D. C., 1937. 29 p.

Odegard, Peter H. and Helms, E. Allen. *American Politics: A Study in Political Dynamics.* New York, Harpers, 1938. 896 p.

Pulliam, Roscoe. "The Influence of the Federal Government in Education," *School and Society,* 47:63-74, January 15, 1938.

Rankin, E. R. (comp.). *Federal Aid for Education.* University of North Carolina Extension Bulletin, Vol. 13, No. 2. Chapel Hill, University of North Carolina Press, September, 1942. 89 p.

Richardson, James D. *A Compilation of the Messages and Papers of the Presidents, 1789-1897.* Washington, D. C., Government Printing Office, 1896-1899. 10 vols.

Rives, John C. (ed.). *The Congressional Globe, Containing the Debates and Proceedings of the . . . Session of the . . . Congress.* Washington, D. C., Congressional Globe, 1862-1873.

Schlesinger, Arthur M. *Political and Social Growth of the United States: 1852-1933.* New York, Macmillan, 1937. 564 p.

Shannon, Fred A. *The Farmer's Last Frontier: Agriculture 1860-1897* (Vol. V. The Economic History of the United States). New York, Farrar and Rinehart, 1945. 434 p.

Shields, Thomas Edward. *Philosophy of Education.* Washington, D. C., Catholic Education Press, 1917. 446 p.

Smalley, Eugene V. *A Brief History of the Republican Party.* New York, Alden, 1888. 156 p.

Swift, Fletcher Harper. *Federal Aid to Public Schools.* U. S. Department of Interior, Bureau of Education Bulletin No. 47, Washington, D. C., Government Printing Office, 1923. 47 p.

Swift, Fletcher Harper. *A History of Public Permanent Common School Funds in the United States, 1795-1905.* New York, Holt, 1911. 493 p.

Taylor, Harry C. *The Educational Significance of the Early Federal Land Ordinances.* New York, Teachers College, Columbia University, 1922. 138 p.

United States Department of Interior, Bureau of Education. *A Handbook of Educational Associations and Foundations in the United States.* Bureau of Education Bulletin No. 16, Washington, D. C., Government Printing Office, 1926. 82 p.

United States Department of Interior, General Land Office. *School Lands: Land Grants to States and Territories for Educational and Other Purposes.* General Land Office Informational Bulletin Series No. 1, Washington, D. C., Government Printing Office, 1939.
United States Congress. *Biographical Directory of the American Congress, 1774-1927.* Sixty-Ninth Congress, Second Session, House Document No. 783, Washington, D. C., Government Printing Office, 1928. 1740 p.
United States Congress. *Congressional Record.* Washington, D. C., Government Printing Office, 1873 to date.

II

Adams, Francis. *The Free School System of the United States.* London, Chapman and Hall, 1875. 309 p.
Alvord, J. W. *Third Semi-Annual Report on Schools for Freedmen.* Bureau of Refugees, Freedmen, and Abandoned Lands, Washington, D. C., Government Printing Office, 1868. 37 p.
Atherton, George W. "The Legislative Career of Justin S. Morrill," *Report of the Commissioner of Education for the Year 1899-1900.* Washington, D. C., Government Printing Office, 1901. pp. 1321-35.
Barnard, Henry. "The State and Education," *American Journal of Education,* 13:717-724, 1863.
Buckham, Matthew H., address of. *Justin Smith Morrill—Centenary Exercises Celebrated by the State of Vermont at Montpelier, April Fourteenth, 1910.* Fulton, N. Y., Morrill Press, 1910. 72 pp.
Cole, Arthur C. *The Irrepressible Conflict: 1850-1865 (A History of American Life,* Vol. VII). New York, Macmillan, 1934. 468 p.
"The Department of Education at Washington, 1867-1870," *American Journal of Education,* 30:193-99, 1880.
Harris, William T. "Establishment of the Office of the Commissioner of Education of the United States, and Henry Barnard's Relation to It," *Report of the Commissioner of Education for the Year 1902,* Vol. I. Washington, D. C., Government Printing Office, 1903. pp. 901-26.
Howard, O. O. *Report of the Commissioner of the Bureau of Refugees, Freedmen, and Abandoned Lands.* Washington, D. C., Government Printing Office, November 1, 1866. 47 p.
James, Edmund J. *The Origin of the Land Grant Act of 1862 and Some Account of Its Author, Jonathan B. Turner.* University of Illinois Studies, Vol. IV, No. 1, Urbana-Champaign, Illinois, University Press, 1910. 111 p.
Johnson, William Cost. *Speech of William Cost Johnson on Public Lands for Educational Purposes, House of Representatives.* Washington, D. C., Gales and Seaton, 1838. 48 p.
Kandel, I. L. *Federal Aid for Vocational Education; A Report to the Carnegie Foundation for the Advancement of Teaching.* Bulletin No. 10, New York, 1917. 127 p.
Mumford, Frederick B. *The Land Grant College Movement.* University of Missouri College of Agriculture, Columbia, Missouri, 1940. 140 p.
"National Education," *American Education Monthly,* 1:19-20, January, 1864.
New York *Evening Post,* January-June, 1866; January-March, 1867.

New York *Herald*, January-June, 1866.

New York *Times*, January-June, 1866; January-March, 1867.

New York *Tribune*, January-March, June, 1866; February-March, 1867.

Parker, William B. *The Life and Public Services of Justin Smith Morrill.* Boston, Houghton Mifflin, 1924. 378 p.

Peirce, Paul S. *The Freedmen's Bureau: A Chapter in the History of Reconstruction.* State University of Iowa Studies in Sociology, Economics, Politics, and History, Vol. III, No. 1, Iowa City, Iowa, 1904. 200 p.

Proceedings of the National Union Republican Convention Held at Chicago, May 20 and 21, 1868. Chicago, Evening Journal Printers, 1868. 143 p.

Rickoff, Andrew Jackson. "A National Bureau of Education," *National Teachers' Association, Proceedings and Lectures of the Fifth Annual Meeting.* Hartford, American Journal of Education, 1865. pp 299-310.

Russell, John Dale. "The Evolution of the Present Relations of the Federal Government to Education in the United States," *The Journal of Negro Education*, 7:244-55, July, 1938.

Shiras, Alex. *The National Bureau of Education* (prepared under the direction of the Commissioner of Education). Washington, Government Printing Office, 1875. 16 p.

Smith, Darrell H. *The Bureau of Education: Its History, Activities, and Organization.* Institute for Government Research, Service Monograph of the U. S. Government No. 14, Baltimore, Johns Hopkins Press, 1923. 157 p.

Steiner, Bernard C. *Life of Henry Barnard.* U. S. Department of Interior, Bureau of Education, Bulletin No. 8, Washington, D. C., Government Printing Office, 1919. 127 p.

United States Department of Interior, Bureau of Education. *Analytical Index to Barnard's American Journal of Education.* Washington, D. C., Government Printing Office, 1892. 128 p.

United States Bureau of Freedmen and Refugees. *Report of the Hon. T. D. Eliot, Chairman of the Committee on Freedmen's Affairs to the House of Representatives, March 10, 1868.* Washington, D. C., Government Printing Office, 1868. 32 p.

White, Emerson E. "National Bureau of Education," *American Journal of Education*, 16:177-86, 1866.

III

Carthage, Illinois, *Gazette*, 1871.

Eaton, John. *The Relation of the National Government to Public Education.* Cleveland, National Teachers' Association, 1870. 13 p.

"Education in Congress," *National Quarterly Review*, 14:159-69, December, 1866.

"The Educational Question," *The Catholic World*, 9:121-35, April, 1869.

Gillett, Frederick, H. *George Frisbie Hoar.* Boston, Houghton Mifflin, 1934. 311 p.

Hoar, George F. *Autobiography of Seventy Years.* New York, Scribners, 1903. 927 p.

Hoar, George F. "Education in Congress," *Old and New*, 5:599-605, May, 1872.

Proceedings of the National Association of School Superintendents at a Special Session at Washington, D. C. New York, A. S. Barnes, March, 1870. 19 p.

"The National Bureau of Education," *The Educational Journal of Virginia,* 2:119, January, 1871.

National Education Association of the United States. *The Addresses and Journal of Proceedings of the National Educational Association, Sessions of the Year 1871* at St. Louis, Mo. New York, James H. Holmes, 1871, 235 p.

New York *Evening Post,* June, 1870; January-February, 1871.

New York *Herald,* January-February, 1871.

New York *Times,* January-February, June, 1870; January-February, 1871.

New York *Tribune,* January-February, June, 1870; January-February, 1871.

"Our Miscellany," *Education Journal of Virginia,* 2:109, January, 1871.

Petersburg, Virginia, *Daily Index,* January-June, 1870; January-February, 1871.

Providence *Daily Journal,* January-February, 1871.

"Reviews and Literary Notices," *Atlantic Monthly,* 26:639-40, November, 1870.

San Francisco *Bulletin,* January-February, 1871.

"Topics of the Times: Compulsory Education," *Scribner's Monthly,* 2:94-96, 1871.

"Unification and Education," *Catholic World,* 13:1-14, April, 1871.

United States Department of Interior, Bureau of Education. *Report of the Commissioner of Education Made to the Secretary of the Interior for the Year 1870.* Washington, D. C., Government Printing Office, 1875. 579 p.

United States Department of Interior, Bureau of Education. *Report of the Commissioner of Education for the Year 1871.* Washington, D. C., Government Printing Office, 1872. 715 p.

Warren, Charles. *Illiteracy in the United States in 1870 and 1880, with Diagrams and Observations.* U. S. Bureau of Education Circular No. 3, Washington, D. C., Government Printing Office, 1884. 99 p.

Warsaw, Illinois, *Bulletin,* 1871.

Wilson, Henry. "New Departure of the Republican Party," *Atlantic Monthly,* 27:104-20, January, 1871.

IV

"A National Educational Fund," *The Republic: A Monthly Magazine Devoted to the Dissemination of Political Information,* 1:34-37, March, 1873.

Barnard, F. A. P. *Education and the State.* New York, S. W. Green, 1879. 65 p.

Blaine, James G. *Twenty Years of Congress: From Lincoln to Garfield.* Norwich, Connecticut, Bill, 1886. 2 vols.

Brownson, Orestes A. "Politics at Home," *Brownson's Quarterly Review,* 1:95-110, January, 1873.

Brownson, Orestes A. "Whose Is the Child?" *Brownson's Quarterly Review,* 1:289-300, July, 1873.

Carthage, Illinois, *Gazette,* 1872.

Cincinnati *Weekly Times,* December, 1880.

Democratic Party National Committee, *The Campaign Text Book.* New York, n.p., 1876. 754 p.

Doty, Duane. *A Statement of the Theory of Education in the United States of America as approved by many leading educators.* Washington, D. C., Government Printing Office, 1874. 22 p.

"Editor's Easy Chair," *Harper's New Monthly Magazine*, 50:131-36, December, 1874.

"Editor's Historical Record: Industrial Education," *Harper's New Monthly Magazine*, 46:624-29, March, 1873.

"Education," *Atlantic Monthly*, 37:126-28, January, 1876.

"Education," *Atlantic Monthly*, 37:252-56, February, 1876.

Eliot, Charles W. "A National University," *Popular Science Monthly*, 3:689-92, October, 1873.

Eliot, Charles W. *A National University.* Cambridge, Sever, 1874. 23 p.

Proceedings of the Seventh Annual Meeting of the Georgia Teachers' Association, 1873. Atlanta, Constitution, 1874. 168 p.

Henderson, John C. Jr. *Our National System of Education.* New York, Dodd-Mead, 1877. 136 p.

Hinsdale, B. A. *Our Common-School Education.* Cleveland, Robison, Savage, 1877. 38 p.

Hinsdale, B. A. *President Garfield and Education.* Boston, Osgood, 1882. 433 p.

Lawrence, Eugene. "The First Century of the Republic: Educational Progress," *Harper's New Monthly Magazine*, 51:845-56, November, 1875.

Louisville, Kentucky, *Courier-Journal*, December, 1880.

National Education Association. *The Addresses and Journal of Proceedings of the National Education Association, Sessions of the Year(s) 1872-1880.* Various places of publication.

New York *Times*, January-February, 1872; December, 1880.

New York *Tribune*, January-February, 1872; December, 1880.

New York *World*, December, 1880.

Northrop, B. G. *Schools and Communism, National Schools, and Other Papers.* New Haven, Tuttle, Morehouse and Taylor, 1879. 80 p.

One Hundred Reasons Why Every Man Should Vote for the Reelection of President Grant. n.p., 1872. 8 p.

"Our Educational Outlook," *Scribner's Monthly*, 4:97-103, 1872.

Periam, Jonathan. *The Groundswell: A History of the Origins, Aims, and Progress of the Farmers' Movement.* Cincinnati, Hanneford, 1874. 576 p.

Politics and the School Question: Attitude of the Republican and Democratic Parties in 1876. n.p., n.d. 15 p.

Providence *Daily Journal*, January-February, 1872; March-April, 1879; December, 1880.

The Republican Party the Workingman's Friend. n.p. 1872 (?), 8 p.

Proceedings of the National Union Republican Convention Held at Philadelphia, June 5 and 6, 1872. Washington, D. C., Gibson Brothers, 1872.

"The Rights of the Church Over Education," *Catholic World*, 21:721-41, September, 1875.

San Francisco *Evening Bulletin*, January-February, 1872; December, 1880.

United States Department of Interior. *Report of the Secretary of the Interior, Being Part of the Message and Documents Communicated to the Two*

Houses of Congress at the Beginning of the Second Session of the Forty-Second Congress, Vol. II: Report of the Commissioner of Education. Washington, D. C., Government Printing Office, 1872. 715 pp.

"Who Is to Educate Our Children?" *Catholic World,* 14:433-47, January, 1872.

V AND VI

Allen, E. A. *Labor and Capital.* n.p., 1891. 536 p.

American Bankers' Association. *First Report of the Executive Council of the American Bankers' Association for the Year 1877.* New York, Evening Post, 1877.

American Bankers' Association. *Reports of the Proceedings at Conventions of the American Bankers' Association From Its Organization in 1875 to 1889.* New York, Bankers Publishing Association, 1890. 2 vols.

American Federation of Labor. *Labor and Education.* American Federation of Labor, 1939. 77 p.

American Federation of Labor. *Report of the Proceedings of the Second Annual Session of the American Federation of Labor Held in Baltimore, Maryland, December 13 to 17, 1887.* New York, 1887. 32 p.

American Federation of Labor. *Report of Proceedings of the Third Annual Convention of the American Federation of Labor Held at St. Louis, Mo., December 11, 12, 13, 14, and 15, 1888.* Philadelphia, 1889. 36 p.

American Federation of Labor. *Report of Proceedings of the Ninth Annual Convention of the American Federation of Labor Held at Boston, Mass., December 10, 11, 12, 13, and 14, 1889.* Philadelphia, 1890. 46 p.

Beath, Robert B. *History of the Grand Army of the Republic.* New York, Bryan, Taylor and Co., 1889. 702 p.

Bergh, Albert E. (ed.). *Letters and Addresses of Grover Cleveland.* New York, Unit, 1909. 499 p.

Birmingham, Alabama, *Age (Age-Herald),* February 13, 1886; December 19, 1889.

Blair, Henry W. (ed.). *The Education Bill.* New York, American News Co., 1887. 52 p.

Bloom, S. S. *Why We Are Democrats; or The Principles and Policies of The American Democracy.* Chicago, Belford, Clarke, 1883. 235 p.

Boston, *Herald,* February 9, 1886.

Boston *Journal,* February 18, 1886.

Boston *Traveler,* February 18, 1886.

Chamberlain, Daniel H. "Present Aspects of the Southern Question." *New Englander and Yale Review,* 9:26-33, January, 1886.

The Churchman (untitled editorials), 53:228-29, February 27, 1886, and 57:248-9, March 3, 1888.

Cincinnati *Weekly Times,* March-April, 1884.

"Congress and National Aid," *Journal of Education* (Boston), 23:41, January 21, 1886.

Curry, J. L. M. "National Aid to Education." U. S. Department of Interior, *Bureau of Education Circular No. 3,* Washington, D. C., Government Printing Office, 1884. pp. 89-99.

Curry, J. L. M. *National Problem of Southern Education.* Richmond, Dispatch, 1882. 16 p.

Dawson, George F. (ed.). *The Republican Campaign Text Book for 1888.* New York, Brentano's, 1888, 250 p.

Democratic Congressional Committee. *The Campaign Book(s) of the Democratic Party.* Washington, Polkinhorn, 1882 and 1886. 222 and 295 p.

National Democratic Committee. *The Campaign Text Book.* New York, n.p., 1880. 557 p.

National Democratic Committee. *The Political Reformation of 1884, A Democratic Campaign Book.* New York, n.p., 1884. 302 p.

Democratic National Committee. *The Campaign Text Book of the Democratic Party for the Presidential Election of 1888.* New York, Brentano's, 1888. 656 p.

Dickinson, J. W. "National Aid for Public Schools," *Journal of Education* (Boston), 18:227-28, October 11, 1883.

Dunning, N. A. *The Farmers' Alliance History and Agricultural Digest.* Washington, D. C., Alliance, 1891. 742 p.

Eaton, John. "The Nation, The Only Patron of Education Equal to the Present Emergency," *Education*, 4:333-45, March, 1884.

Edgar, George P. *Both Sides of the School Question.* New York, Holt, 1880. 16 p.

"Education Bills Before Congress," *New Princeton Review*, 2:131-34, July, 1886.

"False Friendship to the South," *The Critic*, 8:265-69, May 29, 1886.

"Federal Aid to Education," *New Princeton Review*, 1:210-18, March, 1886.

Federation of Organized Trades and Labor Unions of the United States and Canada. *Report(s) of the First (and) Fourth Annual Session(s) . . . 1881 (and) 1884.* Cincinnati, Washington, 1882 and 1884. 24 p. and 36 p.

Grand Army of the Republic. *Journal of the* (Twentieth to Twenty-Fourth) *Annual Session(s) of the National Encampment*, 1886 to 1891.

Hartzell, J. C. (ed.). *Christian Educators in Council: Sixty Addresses by American Educators, National Education Assembly, August 1883.* New York, Phillips and Hunt, 1884. 266 p.

Hartzell, J. C. "The Problem of Education in the Southern States," *Methodist Review*, 64:39-50, January, 1892.

Hawkins, Dexter A. "National Aid to State Common School Education." U. S. Department of Interior, *Bureau of Education Circular No. 2*, Washington, D. C., Government Printing Office, 1882. pp. 48-55.

Haygood, Atticus G. "If Universal Suffrage, Then Universal Education." U. S. Department of Interior, *Bureau of Education Circular No. 3*, Washington, D. C., Government Printing Office, 1883. pp. 43-54.

Haygood, Atticus G. "The South and the School Problem," *Harper's*, 79:225-31, July, 1889.

Hinsdale, Burke A. "Documents Illustrative of American Educational History." U. S. Department of Interior, Bureau of Education, *Report of the Commissioner of Education for the Year 1892-93*, Washington, D. C., Government Printing Office, 1893. Vol. II, pp. 1225-1414.

Hinsdale, B. A. "What Is the Mission of the Common School?" *Journal of Education* (Boston), 18:179-80, September 20, 1883.

Hogg, Alex. "Federal Aid," *Journal of Education* (Boston), 17:148-49, March 8, 1888.

Holt, J. Allen. "National Aid to Education—A Reply," *Century*, 28:156-57, May, 1884.

Ingalls, John James. "National Aid to Common Schools," *North American Review*, 142:381-86, April, 1886.

Inter-State Educational Commission on Federal Aid to Education. *Federal Aid to Education: A Bill to Provide a Fund of $65,737,290 . . . With Tables, etc.* Boston, 30 Franklin St., December 29, 1883. 16 p.

James, E. J. "National Aid to Popular Education," *Andover Review*, 5:250-62, March, 1886.

Jay, John. "The Nation and the Schools," a letter to the New York *Tribune*, February 20, 1888.

Jenkins, C. N. "A Plea for National Aid to Education," *Century*, 30:810-11, September, 1885.

Journal of Education, (untitled editorial), 15:25-26, January 12, 1882.

Program of Kansas State Teachers' Association to Be Held at Topeka, December 28 to 30, 1885. Topeka, Crane, 1885. 15 p.

Louisville, Kentucky, *Courier-Journal*, March, July, 1882; January-February, 1883.

Lovett, J. A. B. "Federal Aid." U. S. Department of Interior, *Bureau of Education Circular No. 6*, Washington, D. C., Government Printing Office, 1888. pp. 146-48.

McPherson, Edward. *A Handbook of Politics for 1886.* Washington, D. C., Chapman, 1886. 247 p.

Marble, A. P. "The Blair Bill." U. S. Department of Interior, *Bureau of Education Circular of Information No. 6*, Washington, D. C., Government Printing Office, 1888. pp. 148-152.

Mayo, A. D. "National Aid for Education," *Journal of Education* (Boston) 16:117-18, August 24, 1882.

Mayo, A. D. "Robert Charles Winthrop and the Peabody Education Fund for the South." U. S. Department of Interior, Bureau of Education, *Report of the Commissioner of Education for the Year 1893-94*, Vol. I, Washington, D. C., Government Printing Office, 1896. pp 739-71.

"National Aid," *The School Journal*, 31:180, March 20, 1886.

"National Aid to Education," *The School Journal*, 31:116, February 20, 1886.

National Education Association. *The Journal of Proceedings and Addresses of the National Education Association of the United States of the Year(s) 1881 (to 1891)*, various places of publication.

"The National Government and Education," *Harper's New Monthly Magazine*, 68:471-76, February 1884.

Nevins, Allan. *The Evening Post; A Century of Journalism.* New York, Boni and Liveright, 1922, 590 p.

New Orleans *Daily Picayune*, February 13, 1886.

New York *Evening Post. A Bill to Promote Mendicancy: Facts and Figures Showing That the South Does Not Need Federal Aid for Her Schools* (A reprint of editorials on this subject published in the New York *Evening Post* during January, February, and March, 1886). New York, Evening Post, 1886. 20 p.

New York *Evening Post, A Bill to Promote Mendicancy* (A reprint of editorials on this subject published in the New York *Evening Post* during the years 1886 and 1887). New York Evening Post, 1888. 27 p.

New York *Star*, January 14, 1890.

New York *Sun*, February 1888; February-March, 1890.

New York *Times*, March, July, 1882; January-February, 1883; March-April, 1884; February-March, 1886; February 1888; February-March, 1890.

New York *Tribune*, March, July, 1882; January-February, 1883; March-April, 1884; February, 1888.

New York *World*, March, July, 1882; January-February, 1883; March-April, 1884.

Orcutt, Hiram. "The National Peril," *Journal of Education* (Boston), 23:3-4, January 7, 1886.

Ouida, "The State as an Immoral Teacher," *North American Review*, 153: 193: 204, August, 1891.

Patterson, J. W. "National Aid to Education," *Education*, 1:413-24, May, 1881.

Pierce, Bessie L. *Public Opinion and the Teaching of History*. New York, Knopf, 1926. 380 p.

Peterson, J. B. "National Aid to Education," *Century*, 28:790-92, March, 1884.

"The Political Situation," *New Princeton Review*, 1:62-77, January, 1886.

Portsmouth, Virginia, *Enterprise*, December 18, 1887.

Republican Congressional Committee. *The Republican Campaign Text Book(s) for 1880 (and) 1882*. Washington, D. C., 1880 and 1882. 215 p. and 240 p.

Republican National Committee. *The Republican Campaign Text Book for 1884*. New York, 1884. 235 p.

Republican National Committee. *Republican Platform (1884), Portraits and Sketches of the Lives of Jas. G. Blaine and John A. Logan*. Philadelphia Avil, 1884, 46 p.

Richmond, Virginia, *Whig*, March, July, 1882; January-February, 1883; March-April, 1884; February-March, 1886.

Rollins, G. W. "National Aid to Southern Education," *Academy; A Journal of Secondary Education*, 1:64-65, March, 1886.

Salt Lake City *Daily Tribune*, March-April, 1884; February-March, 1886.

San Francisco *Bulletin*, March, July, 1882; January-February, 1883; March-April, 1884; February, 1888.

Schlesinger, Arthur M. *The Rise of the City: 1878-1898 (A History of American Life*, Volume X). New York, Macmillan, 1938. 494 p.

Scudder, Horace E. "The Church, The State, and The School," *Atlantic Monthly*, 63:786-93, June, 1889.

Shea, J. G. "Federal Schemes to Aid Common Schools in the Southern States," *American Catholic Quarterly Review*, 13:345-59, April, 1888.

Sherman, John. *Recollections of Forty Years in the House, Senate, and Cabinet*. Chicago, Werner, 1895. 2 vols.

Smith, Edwin Burritt. *Education in the South: National Aid*. Chicago, n.p. 1888. 16 p.

Proceedings of the Department of Superintendence of the National Education Association at Its Meeting in Washington, March 15-17, 1887. U. S. Department of Interior, Bureau of Education Circular of Information No. 3, Washington, D. C., Government Printing Office, 1887. 200 p.

Thwing, C. F. "The National Government and Education," *Harper's New Monthly Magazine*, 68:471-76, February, 1884.

"Topics of the Times: Practical Education in the Common Schools," *Century*, 24:297-99, June, 1882.

The Union League Club of New York. New York, Putnam, 1888. 104 p.

United States Department of Interior, Bureau of Education. *Report(s) of the Commissioner of Education for the Year(s) 1880 (-1890).* Washington, D. C., Government Printing Office, 1881-1891.

"The Week," *Nation*, 38:305, April 10, 1884.

Wilson, William L. *The Tariff* (reprint of a speech in the House of Representatives, May 3, 1888). New York, n.p. 1888. 19 p.

Wilmington, Delaware, *Evening Journal*, 1890.

Wilson, H. H. "The State as an Educator," *Popular Science Monthly*, 18: 664-69, March, 1881.

PERIODICALS CITED

A listing of all magazines, journals, and association organs which were consulted and used in the course of this investigation. The dates following each citation indicate the period for which the periodical was surveyed.

Academy: A Journal of Secondary Education (Associated Academic Principals of the State of New York). Syracuse, George A. Bacon. 1886-1890.

American Catholic Quarterly Review. Philadelphia, Hardy and Mahony. April, 1888.

American Educational Monthly. New York, Schermerhorn, Bancroft and Co. 1864-1876.

American Federationist. New York, American Federation of Labor. 1894.

American Journal of Education. Hartford, Henry Barnard. 1860-1882.

Andover Review. Boston, Houghton Mifflin. 1884-1893.

Atlantic Monthly. Boston, Fields, Osgood and Co. 1866-1890.

Brownson's Quarterly Review. New York, Fr. Pustet. 1871-1873.

Catholic World: A Monthly Magazine of General Literature and Science. New York, Catholic Publishing Society. 1865-1891.

Century Magazine—see *Scribner's Monthly.*

Churchman. New York, Mallory and Co. 1886-1888.

Critic. New York, Critic and G. P. Putnam and Co. 1885-1890.

Education. Boston, New England Publishing Co. 1880-1890.

Educational Journal of Virginia. Richmond, 1869-1871.

Harpers' New Monthly Magazine. New York, Harper and Brothers. 1866-1890.

Journal of Education. Boston, Bicknell. 1880-1890.

Journal of Negro Education, Washington, D. C., Howard University College of Education. July, 1938.

Massachusetts Teacher: A Journal of School and Home Education. Boston, Massachusetts Teachers' Association. 1866-1872.

Methodist Review. New York, Hunt and Eaton. January, 1892.

Michigan Teacher; Organ of the State Teachers' Association and the Department of Public Instruction. Ypsilanti. 1866-1870.

Nation. New York, Evening Post Publishing Co. 1865-1890.

National Quarterly Review. New York, National Quarterly Review. 1860-1880.

National Teacher: a Monthly Educational Journal. Columbus, Ohio, E. E. White, 1870-1873.

New Englander and Yale Review. New Haven, Kingsely, 1866-1885.

New Princeton Review. New York, A. C. Armstrong and Sons. 1886-1891.

North American Review. New York, 30 Lafayette Place. 1866-1891.

Ohio Educational Monthly: the Organ of the Ohio Teachers' Association and the Commissioner for Common Schools. Columbus, Jenkins. 1865-1872.

Old and New. Boston, Roberts Brothers, 1870-1875.

Pennsylvania School Journal. Lancaster, Inquirer. 1866-1872.

Political Science Quarterly. New York, Columbia University. 1889-1891; 1920.

Popular Science Monthly. New York, Appleton. 1872-1891.

Railway Age for the Year(s) 1877 (to 1890). Chicago, Railway Age. 1877-1890.

Republic: A Monthly Magazine Devoted to the Dissemination of Political Information. Washington, D. C., Republic. 1873.

School and Society. New York, Science Press. 1938.

School Journal. New York, E. L. Kellogg Co. 1881-1890.

Scribner's Monthly. New York, Scribner. 1870-1890.

PERIODICALS CONSULTED

A listing of the magazines, journals, and association organs or other records which were consulted but not specifically cited or used in the course of this investigation. The dates following each citation indicate the period for which the periodical was surveyed.

American Association for the Advancement of Science. *Proceedings.* 1875, 1877-1888.

American Journal of Education. St. Louis, Merwin. 1884-1890.

Arkansas School Journal. Little Rock. 1880-1883.

Association of American Agricultural Colleges and Experiment Stations. *Proceedings of the First Annual Convention.* Burlington, Vermont. 1887.

Association of Collegiate Alumnae. *Register.* 1889-90, n.p., n.d.

Association of Friends of Free Instruction of Adult Colored Persons. *Annual Report.* Philadelphia. 1858-1863.

Barnes' Educational Monthly. New York, n.p. 1874-1877.

California Teachers' Association. *The California Teacher.* San Francisco, Bacon and Co. 1864-1868.

Chautauquan. Meadville, Pennsylvania, Teho. L. Flood. 1880-1890.

Child Study Association of America, *Report.* New York. 1890.

Christian Observer. Louisville, Kentucky, n.p. 1869-1891.

Christian Union. New York, Christian Union Co. 1889-1890.

Christian Educator. Cincinnati, n.p. 1889-1890.

College Association of Pennsylvania, *History of the Organization and the Proceedings of the First (to Fourth) Convention.* Lippincott. 1887-1890.

Contemporary Review. New York, Alexander Strahan. 1865-1891.

Cosmopolitan. Rochester, New York, n.p. 1886-1890.

Every Saturday. Boston, James B. Osgood Co. 1866-1874.

Forum. New York, Forum Publishing Co. 1886-1890.

Illinois State Teachers' Association, *Illinois School Journal.* n.p. 1882-1888.

Indiana School Journal. Indianapolis. 1866-1890.

Land We Love. Richmond, Virginia, D. H. Hill. 1866-1869.

Littell's Living Age. Boston, E. Littell and Co. 1866-1891.

New Eclectic (Southern Magazine after 1871). Baltimore, Murdock, Browne and Hill. 1868-1875.

New England Association of Colleges and Preparatory Schools, *Addresses and Proceedings.* Boston, New England Association. . . . 1892.

New Hampshire State Teachers' Association, *New Hampshire Journal of Education.* Concord. 1859-1862.

Primary Teacher. Boston, Bicknell. 1878-1890.

Public School Journal. Bloomington, Illinois, n.p. 1889-1890.

Rhode Island Schoolmaster. Providence, n.p. 1867-1874.

Texas State Teachers' Association, *Minutes of the Eleventh Annual Session.* n.p. 1890.

Wisconsin State Journal: The Official State Paper. Madison, Atwood and Culver. 1871-1872.

Women's Educational and Industrial Union, *Annual Report.* Boston, n.p. 1878-1891.

INDEX